Expl

Successful

Entrepreneurship

"Bringing Your God-Given Gift To The Surface For Success!"

ANN HANEY

Aaron Publishing
Shelbyville, TN
37160

www.annhaney.com

Printed in the United States of America

First Printing, March 2012

ISBN 0-9702265-7-8

Published by
Aaron Publishing
225 Peacock Lane
Shelbyville, TN 37160

Dedication

This book is dedicated to God first and foremost for the grace and favor He has given me and for His unfailing love that never gave up on me. To my husband and my six beautiful children I am also indebted. My husband has always worked hard to support our family so I could remain a stay at home mom and develop a home business and ministry. To my children I credit much laughter, love and teamwork for supporting me in my speaking and writing. I also express much gratitude to my mother for helping teach when I had speaking engagements and my father for giving her up for a few hours each time. My accomplishments are truly my family's accomplishments. Last but certainly not least, my two dear friends Anna and Teresa, who have been a constant word of encouragement to me.

Tribute

This book is a tribute to my grandmother and my sister, my heroes of faith, who left a legacy of love and success behind. To my grandmother I owe the gratitude of her investments in ministries of which she gave abundantly to. Through these ministries she developed a collection of Christian materials which greatly impacted my life growing up. Although we may never know how one person's giving can truly impact the life of another, I can say without question that what she left behind in these resources played a major role in where I am today. To my beautiful sister I owe the gratitude of confidence in taking her call to the lives of others through self-sacrifice. My sister boldly shared God in music and word to everyone she met, always putting others before herself. Her confidence has given me the confidence to carry on the legacy she left behind when she went home to be with her Lord.

Foreward

Through much prayer this book has been birthed. It is my desire to bring a word of more than hope—a word of empowerment from God to His people. I believe God has heard the cries of His people and desires in this day and time to deliver them from the bondages of economic hardship and bring them into the blessings of God. As I look around I see so many hurting people who have settled for what life has dealt them while living in poverty and depression. This is not the plan of God for His people. We are to be more than conquerors through Christ, yet many are living more like victims of circumstances. It is time the word goes out that empowers people to become overcomers and achievers. It is time to turn hope into happenings and act upon the word of God in assurance of it's truth!

"The Spirit of the Lord God is upon me, because the Lord has anointed and qualified me to preach the Gospel of good tidings to the meek, the poor, the afflicted; He has sent me to bind up and heal the broken-hearted, to proclaim liberty to the [physical and spiritual captives and the opening of the prison and of the eyes to those who are bound, to proclaim the acceptable year of the Lord [the year of HIS FAVOR] and the day of vengeance of our God, to comfort all who mourn."
Isaiah 61:1-2

Today is the day to take God at His Word and receive victory over your circumstances!

In order to build a prosperous business you must first believe God has equipped you with the ability to do it and that He wants you to be successful. You do this by uncovering the gift God has placed in you and putting it in action to bring an explosion of success in your life. The road to success is not easy, but it is assured when God is leading it.

If you have come from a family of entrepreneurs consider yourself among the blessed. Most people have grown up with the mindset that when high school is complete they will find a part time job, go to college and eventually go on to work somewhere within the workforce. Their hopes become rooted in finding a good paying job they enjoy that will support them the rest of their lives. Is there anything wrong with this you may be wondering? After all we all hope to find a profitable source of income derived from something we enjoy, right? Unfortunately, what I see happening more and more is that the job market is often limited, even with a good college education and most are forced to take what they can find, even if it is not something they enjoy. On top of that most have occurred much debt in paying for the education to receive a job they can't find. Let me reassure you I am not against college, I believe education is the greatest tool we have to success. However, what I do believe is so many have limited their future to the patterns of the past and find themselves struggling through just as their parents did. Children who come from entrepreneur parents only know to start a business, whereas children who come from employed parents only know to get a job. I believe as you read this book you will discover how God has gifted you with a sure found success to abundant life in the present as an entre-preneur.

"I tell you the truth, Jesus replied, no one who has left home or brothers or sisters or mother or father or children or fields for Me and the gospel will fail to receive a hundred times as much now in this time— houses and brothers and sisters and mothers and children and lands, with persecutions-and in the age to come, eternal life."
Mark 10:29-30 [AMP]

What I believe God is telling us here is He must be first if we are going to receive abundance in this lifetime. God has a plan and gifts He has instilled in each of us to accomplish His purpose and we are not to let anything else stand in it's way. We are not to assume the only way to live our life is by follow-ing someone else. We must learn from others but lead from God. It must be mentioned that when we step out to follow God we will face persecutions. It is not the enemies plan for us to live victorious lives. Most people never reach their full abundance in this lifetime due to the persecutions the enemy throws at them. I want to be among the victorious who receive NOW and IN ETERNAL LIFE. How about you?

It is my hope that through this book you will find God's plan for your life discover the gift God has placed in you to make you a leader, an entrepre-neur! May God's blessings abound in your life and may a new generation of Entrepreneurs be birthed.

Contents

CHAPTER 1

Are You Sure
I Have A Gift?

Do you believe God had a plan for your life before you were ever born? He did! You see God perfectly designed you, your character, disposition, talents and everything about you. He has a plan for your life no one else can accomplish and He desires to see you fulfill it completely to bring abundance to you and glory to Him. Not only did God have plans, He had "Holy Plans." Holy refers to that of a divine power. This means that the plans God has for you are equipped with His power to accomplish what He desires.

"Before I shaped you in the womb, I knew all about you. Before you saw the light of day, I HAD HOLY PLANS FOR YOU."
Jeremiah 1:5

The Importance of God's Gift—

We can easily see now that God truly has a specific plan for our life, but how do we go about fulfilling the plan He has? Let's use an example to see how this fulfillment can come about.

My Plan—Make apple pie
Needed Ingredients—apples, flour, sugar, butter, pie crusts.
Procedure— Mix the ingredients & pour into the pie crusts. Bake until done. Enjoy!

What do you notice about our plan? In order to complete our plan the proper ingredients must be used. When God establishes a plan for our lives He fills us with all the ingredients (gifts) to fulfill His plan.

"There are distinctive varieties and distributions of gifts, (extraordinary powers distinguishing certain Christians….) and they vary, but the Holy Spirit remains the same."
1 Corinthians 12:4

You see God uses different ingredients (gifts) for different people to bring about different ministries. If we used the same ingredients in all our recipes we would get the same creation every time. God doesn't want all apple pies. Thus, the reason God uses a variety. It takes different types of people to minister to the specific needs of others. Most of the time people who have specific challenges want to hear from someone who has experienced what they are going through and who have became victorious. Let's face it—we all need encouragement at some point in our lives and someone who can't relate to our specific situation can't provide us the encouragement we need. God orchestrates a diversity of gifts to meet the needs of all mankind.

Next, notice the procedure that must take place for the plan to be set in motion. The ingredients must be used together to accomplish the same purpose— producing an apple pie. God also has one purpose when He joins your gifts together—bringing others to Christ.

"Go ye therefore and teach all nations baptizing

them in the name of the Father, Son and Holy Spirit."
Matthew 28:30

Although, God has one specific purpose, He uses a variety of gifts in an individual for the purpose of functioning together to produce His purpose. In producing the pie we need all the ingredients to make it successful. Apples alone will not create a pie. Pie crusts without apples will not produce an apple pie. We must actively use all our gifts together to bring the successfulness we want to achieve. God expects us to combine our gifts and use them where we can be most effective for His kingdom. He will do this by using our gifts to assign us different careers. It is up to us to use them.

"Having gifts (faculties, talents and qualities) that differ according to the grace given us, LET US USE THEM."
Romans 12:6

We can easily look into scripture and see a wide diversity of gifts God used in different people to bring about His purpose for his people during their appointed time.

The facts may be on the table proving we have gifts, but often this is not enough to convince us of their importance. Unfortunately, all too often people do not like the gifts God gives them and they desire the gifts of someone else. Exercising someone else's gift will not bring successfulness to your life. Only when you use your gift will you be a successful entrepreneur. Fighting the gift God gives you brings defeat. God as the master creator does not let us fill out a gift request form. He knows the job He has for you to do and He equips you to do it.

"Does not the potter have the right to make out of the same lump of clay some pottery for noble purposes and some for common use?"
Romans 9:21

Think for a moment about a job that has been posted by a company. The owner determines he has a position that needs filled to bring about growth and successfulness to his company. He takes applications and chooses the candidate who is most qualified for the position based upon their skills and character. What he doesn't do is let the candidate tell him who he must hire for the position. Why? If the candidate wants the position, but lacks the qualifications to do the job, the successfulness and growth of his business will be jeopardized. Needless to say, neither the employee or the employer will benefit from this and much time will be wasted when accomplishments could have been made.

Hindering Mindsets Regarding The Gift—

Generally, the reason people try to work within the giftings of others is due to the fact they minimize the value of their own gift. I see four main reasons why people try to work in the gifts of others. Here is the first one:

1. Their gift seems out of character in their own eyes. Here's an example:

A young man has an exceptional ability to write poetry. His words are full of discernment and produce an amazement to all he allows to hear them. Not only are they full of knowledge they also flow with a conviction to better other's lives. However, the young man feels his gift is not masculine enough and lays down his pen to compose.

History reminds us of Francis Scott Key, whose poem became "The Star Spangled Banner" , the National Anthem. Another great poet whose works became well-known hymns was Thomas Chisholm. He wrote over 1200 poems, many became great hymns, like "Great Is Thy Faithfulness." Truly the impact of these works were great upon our lives. We must wonder, 'what if they didn't use their gift?' Look at the example of the young man whose gift is poetry. What happens to the lives this man was supposed to see changed through the gift God gave him? He may never know till eternity. However, at that time he will see all the lives he would have helped find hope. On the other hand, the one who takes his gift and doesn't discredit it will someday see the lives he changed by allowing God to use his gift. A gift is not to be chosen, but to be exercised for the glory of God and the betterment of others. Withholding your gift will affect your successfulness and the lives of those it was meant to touch.

2. People tend to diminish their gift due to what they believe is a lack of prominence.

We live in a society that desires to look good and cause others to want to be like us. We see this all around us. It is in the business world as people compete for prominent positions. It is in the churches as people compete to out give others. It is in our friend groups as people compete to have the latest styles, best hair, nicest car, and the list goes on and on. This is a huge form of pride that will lead to failure and discouragement. Trying to compete with someone else will never allow you to become the person God called you to be, either in your character or your career.

"Make a careful exploration of who you are and the work you have been given, and then sink yourself into that. Don't be impressed with yourself. Don't compare yourself with others. Each of you must take responsibility for doing the creative best you can with your own life."
Galatians 6:4 (The Message Bible)

Why have we become a society that views success as what we have instead of how we use what we have? God views differently and bases success on how we use what we've been given. This is what makes us accepted and respected by Him. No satisfaction will ever come from a desire to look good only from a desire to be truly good. The truth is without the gifts of everyone working together, our society fails to make the difference it should.

"He makes the whole body fit together perfectly. As each part does its own special work, it helps the other parts grow, so that the whole body is healthy and growing and full of love. "
Ephesians 4:16

The truth of the matter is we all need others to use their gifts to benefit our own. Think for a minute about talented musician who has the gift of producing beautiful music, however, he has no knowledge of how to market his gift so others can benefit from it. Obviously, he needs someone with the gift of marketing to help him reach his audience. His gift has limited potential without the help of a marketer. Now, does this mean your gift can never be successful without others using their gifts? This is not the point I am trying to get across. I believe God has put everything we need to accomplish His purpose for our life within us, however I believe God's desire for His world, is a people working together to achieve even greater benefits than can be achieved independently. The musician will obviously be successful in his endeavors by using his discovered gift, however, he can multiply the effects of his gift when he networks with other gifted people.

3. People feel inadequate to accomplish what God calls them to.

This is a common occurrence among many people. This usually develops from insecurities related to our past. This is seen a lot in broken homes, with the absence of a father or mother while growing up.

Shocking statistics help us understand why so many find themselves with a feeling of inadequacy. Let's look at some of these statistics:

75% of children/adolescents in chemical dependency hospitals are from single-parent families.[1]

1 out of 5 children have a learning, emotional, or behavioral problem due to the family system changing. [2]

More than one half of all youth incarcerated for criminal acts lived in one-parent families when they were children.[3]

63% of suicides are individuals from single parent families [4]

75% of teenage pregnancies are adolescents from single parent homes [5]

Unfortunately, these children will often never find the call God has put upon their life. It is important to help a child realize their acceptance by God and to find their value through Him if they are going to succeed. All too often the love that is lacking in the family environment can negatively impact the future paths taken. Even though many situations can be unchanged, this does not hinder someone from being successful in their God-given gifts when they

1)Center for Disease Control, Atlanta, GA
2)National Center for Health Statistics
3)Children's Defense Fund
4)FBI Law Enforcement Bulletin - Investigative Aid
5)Children in need: Investment Strategies...Committee for Economic Development)

put their confidence in God's ability to work through them and not their own abilities. The pattern of insecurity can be changed as we lean upon God's unfailing love.

There are many examples of great Biblical heroes who grew up without their God given homes. We look at Moses who led God's people from bondage, who grew up under Pharoah's household. When God revealed His purpose for Moses' life Moses' insecurities concerning his ability, due to a speech impediment, caused him to doubt his call and ask God to send someone else.

"Master, please I don't talk well. I've never been good with words, neither before nor after you spoke to me... Oh Master please send someone else!"
Exodus 4:10, 13

Have you ever questioned God's direction because you felt unequipped to complete the task? God uses the poor to confound the wise. (1 Cor. 1:27) When God calls you, He equips you. He may not fix your insecurity, but He will use it to fulfill His purpose. God is not limited by man's inabilities, but rather by man's insubordination.

I can tell you from personal experience, God has called me out of my comfort zone. When I was in Middle School I swore if I ever made it through speech class I would never speak publicly again. You may laugh if you have read my biography telling of the hundreds of motivational presentations I have presented.

What I can tell you is this—when God called me He equipped me. I pray for His courage and ability each time I speak asking for His words to flow through me to bring glory to Him.

What makes it possible for the insecure to become successful? Their faith in God and willingness to let Him use them to fulfill His purpose.

4. People question whether they are too young or too old for God to use their gift at the present time.

Before I convince you of the falsity of this mindset, let me just say, "God can use you no matter what you're age to be successful! Besides that, He needs YOU! How do I know, you may be wondering? Let's take a look at Mary and Elizabeth in the Bible. We see two women who received similar miraculous gifts, at different ages—the birth of a very special child. God used Mary to bring the Savior into the world, when it was a physical impossibility. God also brought forth a child for Elizabeth when she was past the natural age of conception. Something we note about both of these women, was their willing-ness to accept the gift of God and allow it to bring glory to God. Elizabeth's son ,John, prepared the way for the coming Lord which was a great calling. Mary's son, Jesus, prepared the way for us. Both events were important to the plan of God and com-plimented each other. (Luke 1)

Today's successful older entrepreneurs might in-clude Colonel Sanders who started his KFC business when he was 65 years old from his first social

security check. Prior to his death in 1980 his business consisted of 6,000 restaurants and sales of
more than $2 billion dollars. Sylvia Lieberman be-
came an entrepreneur when she was 90 years old
with an award winning book entitled, *"Archibald"s
Swiss Cheese Mountain."* An interesting fact about
both of these entrepreneurs is the fact that each
donated a portion of their proceeds to charities. [1]

What about today's successful young entrepreneurs
you may ask? How about Mark Zuckerberg, who in
2004 at the age of 20, created what we know as
Facebook. Mark began using computers and writing
software when he was in Middle School. Mark is a
multi-billionaire today. Another young success is
found in Sean Belnick, a 14 year old who started an
office chair business called Bizchair.com Sean
started his business with a $500 investment and the
advice of his stepfather, a veteran in office furniture
business. Today Sean's business sells office furniture to Google, Microsoft and more.[1]

The list could go on and on here. Age is not an ex-
cuse for neglecting the gift God has put within you.
It is never God that changes the gift, but rather the
gifted.

Here is a quote concerning age—

> *You are as young as your faith, as old as your doubt; as*
> *young as your self-confidence, as old as your fear; as*
> *young as your hope, as old as your despair.*
> *~Douglas MacArthur.[2]*

[1])www.quotegarden.com
[2])http://thinkexist.com/quotation/people-grow-old-only-by-deserting-their-ideals/347613.html

Maintain a child-like faith, self-confidence and hope in discovering your God-given gift. Vanish doubt, fear, and despair to surface your pre-destined success. God moves in miraculous ways in the young and the old for His glory and your success!

"For we are God's own handiwork (His workmanship), recreated in Christ Jesus, (born anew) that we may do those good works which God predestined (planned beforehand) for us (taking paths which He prepared ahead of time), that we should walk in them (living the good life which He prearranged and made ready for us to live.)"
Ephesians 2:10

Your work has been preplanned by God with paths to follow and walk in that lead to success. It is important to mention here that once we discover our gift we must remember and never forget where it came from and who it belongs to. God must always remain the center of your focus for success.

"It's God's gift from start to finish! We don't play the major role. If we did, we'd probably go around bragging that we'd done the whole thing. No, we neither make nor save ourselves! God does both the making and the saving. He creates each of us by Christ Jesus to join Him in the work He does, the good work he has gotten ready for us to do, work we had better be doing."
Ephesians 2:8-10 (Message bible)

We know God is talking about His free gift of grace we neither created nor can save ourselves with. However, notice we are to take what God has given us and join Him in the work He has made ready for us. To accept God's gift and apply it where He has made ready is to experience a fruitful harvest spiritually, emotionally, economically and physically.

What God establishes God blesses! Trust He knows what He is doing in your life. He knows the character, talents, events, and every detail of your life which He orchestrates to bring about His purpose.

*"Who got things rolling here, got this champion from the east on the move? Who recruited him for his job?....... Who did this? Who made it happen? Who always gets things started? I did. G*OD! I am the first on the scene. I am also the last to leave."
Isaiah 41:2, 4 (Message bible)

God will get you on the move if you let Him. He is calling you to action, recruiting you for the job. He will get you started and bring you to completion on your road to entrepreneurship through using the gifts He gave you.

"And I am convinced and sure of this very thing, that He who began a good work in you will continue Until the day of Jesus Christ (right up to the time of His return), developing (that good work) and perfecting and bringing it to full completion in you."
Philippians 1:6

Be confident in God!

Be assured of your gift!

Be prepared to succeed!

Chapter 2

Discovering Your Gift

This chapter is probably the one you have been looking forward to the most. The truth is this, probably the number one question we all have, "How do I discover the gift God has put in me for His glory and my success?" What a great question! There are many things that God uses to help us discover our gift. Remember we serve a God who has no lack of ideas or ways to implement those ideas into our lives. I want to start by sharing two key scriptures with you assuring you that God will reveal the gift He's placed within you.

"The steps of a [good] man are directed and established by the Lord when He delights in his way [and He busies Himself with his every step]."
Psalm 37:23

Let's begin by understanding what this scripture means to us in regard to discovering our gifts. First of all, we see that we must position ourselves to be in obedience to God's word. This is what makes us a righteous (good) man in the sight of God. Now don't start feeling unworthy of God's blessings here. We all make mistakes and fall short at different times in our lives. We are not talking about a perfect person who has never been disobedient, but rather a person who has a desire for the things of God. God looks upon the heart. Remember the story of David, who made many mistakes; including adultery and premeditated murder. But what did God say of David—

"David, a man about whom God said, 'I have found David son of Jesse, a man after my own heart. He

will do everything I want him to do.'
Acts 13:22

David was a man who found himself frustrated many times and facing failures, but always had an inner desire to do what God had called Him to do. We notice as God delights in our "heart condition" He busies Himself on our behalf to direct every step we make and even establish them according to His plan. So I want to ask you at this point—what is the condition of your heart? Do you truly want to use your gift to glorify God above everything else. When we do this first, then our gift will bring success to our lives as well. When our desires for advancement become second to our desires to please God it is followed by success that manifests itself in our lives. Therefore if God is directing our steps will they not meet with the discovery of our gift? Absolutely!

Let's look at another scripture that takes us one step further into the confirmation of discovering our gift.

"Roll your works upon the Lord [commit and trust them wholly to Him; He will cause your thoughts to become agreeable to His will, and] so shall your plans be established and succeed."
Proverbs 16:3

Obviously we must have a plan we are in action do-ing. If we are not moving nothing can happen. This will require us to determine a direction to proceed in. When we make this plan and determine this di-rection it is crucial we tell God this is the direction we plan to move in and we need his hand to guide us into making any necessary adjustments. In this way we are committing our plan unto Him, trusting that He will make any necessary changes in our direction. How does He do this? By causing our thoughts to become agreeable to His will! This is the only way we can be sure that our gift will surface and be successful. We must develop a plan, commit the plan to God, move forward with the plan and be confident that the opportunities will all be a part of the path to success.

Why do you suppose God doesn't just tell us what to do, where to go, when to go and what will happen when we go? Often we think it would be nice if He said, "On Tuesday of next week you are to open up a book store, selling self-help books and you will be very successful." The simple answer why is the fact that He wants us to see Him move in every step of our lives and remain dependent on Him. God is a jealous God who desires us to continually depend upon Him for the answers to all of our questions as they arise, not depend upon ourselves.

Even with this basis of applied scripture you still may be wondering, "I don't know what to step out towards and try?" Before I give you some guidelines I want to give you a clear definition in the difference between an "entrepreneur" , an "inventor" and an "innovator."

> Inventor—someone who studies and works hard to create something that has not been produced before.

Entrepreneur—someone who organizes and manages usually an existing idea by improving it and combining it with other ideas to create something unique, who assumes the risks of the business. They are owners of their trade.

Innovator—someone who changes the established way of doing things through research into a better way never tried before

An inventor can become an entrepreneur, using their invention to establish a business. Likewise an entrepreneur usually has a pretty good chance of becoming an inventor because existing ideas can cause the entrepreneur to stretch their thinking to create new ideas for success. Almost always an entrepreneur is an innovator, establishing a better way of doing things through experiencing the need for improvement. The following is an example of this:

Ransom E Olds was the inventor of the first automobile in 1864. He was also an entrepreneur who built the first automobile factory Olds Motor Works in Detroit in 1899. Later a great innovator in 1913, Henry Ford, reduced car assembly time in half. [1]

Our gift can lead us into inventing, innovating, and entrepreneurship. There are some things God has positioned in our thinking that give us insight into the gifts we possess. God has created our minds with specific thoughts that He uses to become a gift in action. Let's learn what they are. Your gift usually

[1])"I Love America's Inventions", copyright ©2001 by Gary Grimm & Associates

stems from one of the following things:

1. A Hobby—something you enjoy doing

Examples:

A) Experimenting with hairstyles might lead to a career as a ——**Hairstylist**

B) Socializing with others might lead to a career as a —-**Politician or Speaker**

C) Drawing might lead to a career as a —— **Cartoonist, Graphics Designer, Web Artist, Illustrator, Art Instructor**

D) Love of Music & Instruments might lead to a career as a —-**Music Teacher, Musician, Song Writer, Choir Director, Voice Trainer**

E) Love for dance might lead to a career as a —- **Dance Instructor, Choreographer**

F) Decorating might lead to a career as a —-- **Florist, Party Coordinator**

G) Love of animals might lead to a career as a —- **Veterinarian, Animal Rescue Shelter, Kennel Owner**

H) Sewing might lead to a career as a —-- **Clothing Designer, Seamstress, Alteration Shop Owner, Upholstery Recoverer**

I) Cooking might lead to a career as a —— **Chef, Caterer, Host of a Cooking Show**

J) Photography might lead to a career as a —- **Photographer (sports, wedding, nature, etc...), Videographer**

K) Love of creating with wood might lead to a career as —- **Home Builder, Architect, Wood Working Shop Owner,**

The list could go on and on, but this should give you an idea of different ways you can use your hobby to develop a career as an entrepreneur. The main goal is not to limit yourself. Try things that might take you out of the normal scope of careers. This might be the very thing that gives you a niche in the market and changes your future.

2. A Talent—something others tell you you're good at
> (The same examples in number 1 can be applied to this category as well.)

3. A Need—something that is a problem in need of a solution
> Examples:
> A) Keeping all your records in one easy to access log book—-**Multi-Purpose Planner**
> B) Reducing waste of toothpaste—-**Perfect Portion Squeeze Clip For Tubes of Toothpaste**
> C) Hands free phone calls—- **Bluetooth**
> D) Driving in the rain—- **Windshield Wipers**
> E) Quick cooking—- **Microwave Ovens**
> F) Clothing Lint—-**Lint Roller**
> G) Reducing Cost of Drinks—- **Paper Cups**
> H) Cutting Travel Time—-**Car**

Again, this list could go on and on as well. One thing you need to remember is not to think your idea is too small to make a difference in your success. Notice some of the examples above range from inventing paper cups to cars. Let's look at a simple idea created years ago that is still simplifying

our lives today that is not necessary but has pro-
vided a convenience people can't do without:

*The Flexible Drinking Straw—- invented in the
1930's by Joseph Friedman proved to be the most
successful of 9 patents he held. Over 500 million
flexible straws are sold annually.* [1]

4. An Irritation—something that stirs up frustration
causing you to bring about a change

(The same examples in number 3 can be applied to
this category as well, however I would like to add a
few more.)

A) Lack of preparation for an event might lead
one to a career as an—-**Event Organizer**
B) Uncut lawns might lead to a career as a —-
Lawn Care Business Owner
C) Un-orderly houses might lead to a
career as a —-**Housekeeper, Space Saver
Coordinator, Organization Advisor**
D) Faded Buildings might lead to a career as
a —- **Painter, Commercial Property
Advisor**

We have talked about opportunities within numerous fields of entrepreneurship. One thing I want to
add is this—ALL of these areas possess the opportunity for authoring a self-help book and speaking.
Any field we choose to become an expert in is a
book waiting to be published and a speaking/
teaching opportunity waiting to be scheduled.
Knowledge is valuable and in demand. People want

[1])http://en.wikipedia.org/wiki/Joseph_Friedman

to hear from those who are doing what they hope to do. This also serves as another source of income for the entrepreneur. You should by now be getting the idea that the possibilities for entrepreneurship are endless. Idealistically the best time to start applying entrepreneurial skills is when you are a child. Unfortunately as an adult we have developed a lifestyle that is often hard to change (but not impossible). I want to take a look with you into ways we can develop a mindset of entrepreneurship in our children from the early years.

Children are fast learners and can be taught the value of money at a very early age. Generally by the time a child is 5 they have a pretty good idea of how money works. They usually have discovered this through petitioning their parents for numerous things they desired only to be told, "money doesn't grow on trees" or "Daddy and Mommy do not have the money for that." It doesn't take long for a child to see a problem—lack of money and look for a solution—where do I get more? This is the perfect time to begin encouraging your child to look for ways to make the money they need to buy what they want. Why is this so important to start this while they're young you may be wondering? Simply this, if you show them that the adventures they pursue have benefits they desire, their minds will become open to creating income when they become older as opposed to depending on someone else to supply the income for them. Many parents do not teach children these things. Often I see something that disturbs me greatly and it is this: parents who give their child everything they want without requir-

-ing effort on the child's part. Parent's who do this do not understand they are setting their child up for failure. A child who is not taught to depend upon their God-given abilities for success will depend upon someone else's success and meet failure. Let me give you a couple examples of this. The first one I want to look at comes from Luke 15 regarding the "Prodigal Son". The father had two sons, one demanded his inheritance and blessing from the father immediately. The father agreed and the son lived undisciplined, lavishly and wasted all he had. Times became very hard for the son as he found himself literally eating from the pig pen. The son soon returned home realizing that even the servants of his father were well fed and cared for. This is what happens to the child who is given everything and not made to lead the disciplined life of working for their wages. Fortunately, this story does have a happy ending of the son returning home, but how many of us desire our children to encounter what this son did before he realized the reward of hard work and a disciplined life.

The best love and future stability we can give our children is teaching them self-sufficiency through God-sufficiency as opposed to man obtained sufficiency. Parent's this is a warning you must heed if you don't want to see your child suffer defeat. My second oldest son once told me he couldn't believe all the people he knew his age whose parents gave them everything and how unappreciative they were and boastful of what they had. He went on to say, "I am glad you taught me to work for what I have, because now I know I can do it and don't have to depend on someone else." This is what we want to hear from our children. This is the love that builds the appreciation and sets the stage for a child's future success.

Let me share another story of a man I know who was quite gifted but depended for years on his friendship with another man his age for success. This man worked for years for his friend, an entrepreneur, and one day his friend announced he was closing his business. Although this man was quite talented he was lost on how to use his gift to carry on his financial stability and thus struggled to make ends meet. We must be careful that we do not get so comfortable and fail to fully develop our own gift for our financial future. Our friends are not our future stability no matter how good of friends they are. There is a friend who sticks closer than a brother and He is the only one we can 100% count on for future stability. (Proverbs 18:24)

Let's take a look at some ways we can encourage our child to use their gifts toward becoming an entrepreneur. The first thing you will need to do is ask God to give you insight into your child's unique abilities and talents. God spoke to Zachariah in Luke chapter 1:15-17:

"For He will be great and distinguished in the sight of the Lord and he must not drink wine nor strong drink, and he will be filled with and controlled by the Holy Spirit even in and from his mother's womb. And he will turn back and cause to return many of the sons of Israel to the Lord their

God. And he will go before Him (Jesus) in spirit and power of Elijah, to turn back the hearts of the fathers to the children and the disobedient and incredulous and unpersuadable to the wisdom of the upright in order to make ready for the Lord a people prepared."

Wow! Yes, God does speak to us regarding our child's future. We see here some basic instructions given to Zachariah in preparing him for the gift that God had placed within his son, John. The angel of the Lord also elaborates on what John's call would consist of. I am a firm believer that God will instruct us as parents as to the course to lead our children on in preparing them for the calling God has placed on their life through the use of the gift He has given them. I did this with all my children and as a home school mom I was able to encourage their electives in high school toward their interests and hobbies, which generally evolved around their giftings in some way. This is not to say that if your child attends public school you cannot encourage further learning towards their gift. I believe the important thing here is to make readily available the opportunities to experience their interests and expand them.

Here is a list of some interests/opportunities:

Political Interests— Join debates, write opinionated columns, submit articles to the local paper, start a blog, provide reading materials on historical events, take them to Legislative Day at the state capital, etc..

Video/Photography Interests— Provide reading materials on interest, find a mentor whose interest is the same, enter photography contests, provide photo shoots of nature, animals, etc…, let them do the home videos
(mentors can be friends, pastors, parents, business acquaintances, etc.. Our pastor and a close friend in film making was a great mentor for our son in video)

Making Things—This can be anything from creating recipes in the kitchen, building a GI Joe fort, building a tree swing, building a teepee in the back yard, creating a paper towel tube connecter for the marble to turn off the light switch (don't laugh, this develops a solution finding mind—my son didn't want to turn the light off till he got in bed; he saw a problem and found a solution), blacksmith classes, pottery classes, etc...

Horse Lovers— Make available materials on horse care, grooming the horse, feeding the horse, taking care of the neighbor's horses.

Art Lovers—sign up for art classes, enter art/drawing contests, obtain drawing/painting books for practice and learning, obtain art supplies

For instance, if your child has a love of sports; reading about great sports heroes and enrolling them in sports of interest will further develop their passion and purpose. Encourage them to make money to support their gift. With the above example find ways to allow your child to purchase the bat and glove they have been eyeing for weeks at the store. Help them to think creatively with this. Maybe holding a rummage sale by getting rid of some of the things they have outgrown or grown tired of. Try to encourage them to eBay items to purchase their wants. My 8 year old recently desired to make a purchase and got together one of his toys he had taken good care of and I helped him list it on eBay. He made $70 off of the item and now eBaying is a resource he turns to to strum up that extra cash. Some of my children like to go to rummage sales for the sole purpose of buying things to resale on eBay or Craig's List. Checking out the pawn shops often serve as a source of finding a niche item that is in demand on eBay or Craig's List. It is important if you help your child eBay an item they are taught the responsibility of the listing fee and closing costs that come out of their profit. This is a great way to teach them business principles.

Here is a list of some responsibilities that can turn work to cash and encourage the entrepreneurial mindset:

Raising Chickens & Selling Farm Fresh Eggs
Dog walking & sitting for friends/neighbors
Lemonade Stand (even during a rummage sale)
Vegetable stand (from own garden grown veggies)
Ironing for friends/neighbors
Car Wash
Bake Sale
eBaying outgrown toys or niche items
Taking outgrown clothes to resale shops for cash
Let your child work for your business

It is important to remember that even though your child may be inexperienced, inexperience is the door of opportunity for growth. Never think a child is too young to be taught. We are never too young or too old to obtain knowledge. Our only hindrance is our limited vision of what can be achieved.

Your gift is your trade to success! Gifts are given and trades are achieved. It is important we do not settle for being an overcomer of circumstances, but rather being an achiever above circumstances. An overcomer only strives to make it through their life, while the mindset of the entrepreneur (the achiever) is to take control of their life.

Ask yourself what have I seen in the past, what do we need in the present, and what will impact the future? Learn from history to see what has a history of successfulness and learn why it was successful. Each generation is born anew. Often the past successes are due to be resurrected in the present with innovations for greater success unseen before.

When you discover your gift (the plan of God for your success and His glory) be careful you move with Him for successfulness. At this point our excitement often surpasses His timing. I will discuss this more in chapter 4.

Finally, in closing be proactive in pursuing, perfecting and promoting your gift. It is action that leads to change and change that leads to financial freedom.

Step Up to the Challenge

Step Out in Faith

Step Toward the Call

Step Into Victory

CHAPTER 3

Using Your Gift To Become An Entrepreneur

So what is the big deal about entrepreneurs you may be wondering? Let me sum this up in one simple statement—*Our only true success and happiness will be found in using what God has put in us to bring glory to His name!*

In chapter one we discovered and confirmed the fact that God has indeed given each of us a gift that will benefit our lives and the lives of others. But, couldn't I still operate in this gift without becoming an entrepreneur, you may be thinking? The simple answer is "yes." Let me ask you a question though, "Do you want others to receive the full benefits of your gift, while you receive only a portion? The truth is if you don't use your gift to establish your success someone else will use it to establish theirs. This is not what I believe is God's original purpose for individuals. Now, I am not saying God doesn't want us to benefit others with our gift, but I am saying God doesn't want others to receive more from our gift than we do. What do we know currently about entrepreneurs today?

Non Employer firms steadily increased from 2002-2007 when it hit an all time high of 21,708, 21. In 2008 it began to decrease and in 2009 it stood at 21,090,761.[1] In this book you will discover why people are seeking to become an entrepreneur and why some don't succeed. Unfortunately what I see happening in the job market is quite disheartening. Employers are underpaying those who work for them. Not only are they underpaid, many are on welfare and barely making ends meet.

47

[1] http://censtats.census.gov/cgi-bin/**nonemployer/nonsect.pl**

In 2012 the federal minimum wage requirement was at $7.25 an hour. Four states actually have minimum wages lower than the federal requirement and five have no minimum wage law.[0] Now let's look at what that means for most employees:

At $7.25 hourly 40 hours a week — $1160 month
At $9 hourly 40 hours a week — $1440

Now lets look at how far this will go with the current monthly expenses we are seeing:

Mortgage—-$698[1]
Power—-$118[2]
Water/Sewer—$100
Car Payment—$350[3]
Trash—$20
Phone—$96[4]
Car Insurance— $75[5](liability)
House Insurance—$45[8](minimum)

TOTAL: $1502

Other expenses

Health Insurance—$1100[8](family)
Groceries—$1190[7] (family of 4)
Automobile Gas Expense—$200
(estimated 200 miles weekly with vehicle
getting 15 mpg & gas prices $3.50)

TOTAL: $2490

[0]http://www.dol.gov/whd/minwage/america.htm
[1]Economist outlook national association of realtors (NAR) experts
[2]http://investmentwatchblog.com/electricity-bills-soar-nationwide/
[3]http://www.auto-payment-calculator.com/what-is-the-average-car-payment/
[4]http://money.cnn.com/2011/09/16/pf/how_to_lower_bills.moneymag/index.htm
[5]http://drivesteady.com/average-monthly-cost-of-6-optional-insurance-plans
[7]http://www.cnpp.usda.gov/Publications/FoodPlans/2011/CostofFoodFeb2011.pdf
[8]http://www.insuranceproviders.com/how-much-does-home-insurance-cost-per-month-on-average/

Can you see the problem with what people are being paid? It is sad to think that the government has to make a law requiring employers to pay at least "minimum wage." Shouldn't employers be willing to pay people what they are worth? Obviously, from these figures we can see that it is impossible for people to support themselves more less a family on minimum wage. It is absolutely impossible for a family to make it on this type of income, thus we see more and more families where the husband and wife both work (sometimes even more than one job) and still barely scrimp by. Why do you think this is happening? I can tell you why I believe this is happening—-GREED!

Whoever oppresses the poor to increase his own wealth, or gives to the rich, will only come to poverty.
Proverbs 22:16

The super giant businesses (you can guess who they are—those who don't pay their employees enough to support their basic needs, thus requiring them to apply for welfare) are adding to poverty, while they overpay themselves. People are enslaved to these companies. These large companies have put smaller individually owned companies out of business. We can remember years and years ago when towns thrived on small trade specific businesses. There were shoe stores, flower shops, hometown grocers, book stores, seamstress shops, feed stores, etc... Everyone had a trade and everyone made a living. We have been deceived by these larger companies convincing us they are benefitting

49

the towns economy by bringing in jobs. But, the truth of the matter is this—they have put individuals out of business offering them jobs at minimum wage. Is this helping our communities? If we can each learn to operate in the gift God has given us we will not need to depend upon these "super giants" for support. They claim to give so much funding to schools, charities, etc.., but the truth is it is the employee who is giving to the charities out of their unpaid wages. I am sure you are familiar with the statement "charity begins at home." Should this not be applied to businesses in a sense of—they should take care of their own before helping others? I believe it should. If I decided to take $100 of my earned income and go by groceries for the local food bank, but my children had nothing to eat, would I not be stealing from what is required by God for me to give my children whom I am responsible for?

"Give a bonus to leaders who do a good job….don't muzzle a working ox and a worker deserves his pay."
1 Timothy 4:17-18

In other words don't place limitations on those who work hard. I have heard by so many of the great requirements to produce high quality effort, however the pay remains the same. One instance I have seen was that of an employee who was receiving a pay cut due to the business cutting expenses, however, the duties were increased to bring more success to the business. Is this fair business practice?

Why is it these "super giants" have such a grip on the market? We see this because of their ability to purchase larger quantities (than the smaller business owner) from wholesalers who will sell cheaper to those who buy in bulk. This is just as much an unfair practice by the wholesaler as it is for the "super giant" to make the purchase. Think for a minute about the Apple Corporation whose price is consistent no matter where you buy it. Now, I know we all want a bargain, but what would happen if more companies like Apple would set a standard not to undercut the competition. Obviously, we would see the balance of prosperity amongst all businesses, therefore people could afford it.

"Don't carry around with you two weights, one heavy and the other light, and don't keep two measures at hand, one large and the other small. Use only one weight, a true and honest weight, and one measure, a true and honest measure, so that you will live a long time on the land that God your God is giving you. Dishonest weights and measures are an abomination to God, your God—all this corruption in business deals. "
Deut 25:13-15

I believe this makes it pretty clear. We are to show no favoritism in business. Only when we do this will we have the abundance and blessing of the Lord we were meant to have. What can we do about those who still continue to take advantage of the weaker you may be wondering? Unfortunately, nothing! It is God's job to bring justice upon the unjust. I believe we are starting to see this justice come about. Have you begun to see many of the larger chains closing their doors? Have you been hearing about the financial decline of those who used to be at the top? Yes, we are seeing God's justice come about!

"And God said to Abram, Know positively that your descendants will be strangers dwelling as temporary residents in a land that is not theirs [Egypt], and they will be slaves there and will be afflicted and oppressed for 400 years. And in the fourth generation they [your descendants] shall come back here [to Canaan] again, for the iniquity of the Amorites is not yet full and complete."
Genesis 15:13, 16

We can see clearly God is moving His people out of the bondage again, just as He did years ago. Notice we are the "strangers in Egypt", those who have been in bondage for years to the more powerful taskmasters working for their own gain. However, notice there is a generation that shall enter the Promised Land. We saw the fulfillment of this prophecy when Moses led the people out of bondage and into the Promised Land.

I believe God has heard the cries of His people and is tired of the enemy stealing what is rightfully theirs. People are tired of the bondage that has for far too long kept them scrimping by to find no fruit for their labors. People are ready to leave the bondage in search of the Promised Land.

The wages of the people cry out against the "super giants." God is ready to avenge His people and lead them once again to a land flowing with milk and honey (prosperity).

Behold, the wages of the laborers who mowed your fields, which you kept back by fraud, are crying out against you, and the cries of the harvesters have reached the ears of the Lord of hosts.
James 5:4

The one thing we can do is believe in the gift (ability) God has placed within us and move out of our circumstance and into our success. We are only captive by what we allow ourselves to believe.

People will generally fall in two categories: those who give up and give in to welfare OR those who look for ways to change their circumstances. Since you are reading this book you are probably the person looking for ways to change your circumstances. You are among the people looking for the blessings of God through the gifts He has given you for success. You may still be unsure of God's timing for the use of your gift. Let me give you some insight that might help clear this up for you.

HOW DO I KNOW ITS TIME TO SURFACE MY GIFT FOR SUCCESS?

The confidence to move in the direction you feel led will come through signs God gives you. What are these signs? Let's look at 1 Samuel 10:1-7. This is the story of Saul being called to follow God into what God had planned for him. Samuel tells Saul there will be three signs that confirm his calling.

1st—Two men will meet you and tell you what you have been looking for has been found.

Saul had been greatly worried over how he was going to find the donkey's of his father. Livestock was a source of prosperity in the Bible times and to lose some meant loss of income.

YOUR 1ST SIGN: God will give you peace concerning your financial concerns through revealing a solution.

I have experienced this. I had two major sources of income and marketing ability change at the close of a year. My income had slowed down and I was concerned about how to proceed, whether or not to continue in the same area or to expand my field. I felt God had revealed to me to step out into other areas untried before. At this point God gave me an excited peace regarding my previous concerns and a possible solution to the problem. I felt the Lord telling me to offer myself in other speaking areas through my testimonies of past victories received through the hand of God although I had never done this before.

2nd—Saul was to meet three men who would offer him two loaves of bread.

Saul found provision when he stepped out to follow God's calling and left the past concerns behind.

YOUR 2ND SIGN: God will provide provision to you in regards to the call you have stepped out toward.

Doors of opportunity will open themselves up to you as you step out.

I saw this happen. When I offered myself to speak on these other topics by sending out letters of speaking availability, within 2 hours I received a phone call to speak in several states within the speaking areas I offered.

3rd—Samuel told Saul he would meet with prophets prophesying, then the spirit of the Lord will come on you and you will be prophesying.

YOUR 3RD SIGN: God will send positive people in your life who will stir up the gift that God has put in you. These people will often have a confirming word for you regarding what God has told you.

God brought several people into my life who encouraged the direction I had moved in. A lady gave me a word from God saying, "God was using favor of things from my previous work to bring me into greater things in another direction." How do I know these are signs God often uses to confirm the timing of our gifts action? Look at what Samuel told Saul in regards to what would follow these three signs,

"When these confirming signs are accomplished, you'll know that you're ready: Whatever job you're given to do, do it. God is with you."
1 Samuel 10:7 (Message Bible)

Pray and ask God for direction regarding your financial future. Watch for signs. Disregard human reasoning and act on the opportunities God brings to you. Remember it is at this point that God is with you and moving on your behalf. Don't procrastinate and wait for another answer.

Do you remember the story of the man who prayed for God to save him from drowning?

It had been raining for days and days, and a terrible flood had come over the land. The waters rose so high that one man was forced to climb onto the roof of his house. As the waters rose higher and higher, a man in a rowboat appeared, and told him to get in. "No," replied the man on the roof. "I have faith in the Lord; the Lord will save me." So the man in the rowboat went away. The man on the roof prayed for God to save him. The waters rose higher and higher, and suddenly a speedboat appeared. "Climb in!" shouted a man in the boat. "No," replied the man on the roof. "I have faith in the Lord; the Lord will save me." So the man in the speedboat went away. The man on the roof prayed for God to save him. The waters continued to rise. A helicopter appeared and over the loudspeaker, the pilot announced he would lower a rope to the man on the roof. "No," replied the man on the roof. "I have faith in the Lord; the Lord will save me." So the helicopter went away. The man on the roof prayed for God to save him. The waters rose higher and higher, and eventually they rose so high that the man on the roof was washed away, and alas, the poor man drowned. Upon arriving in heaven, the man marched straight over to God. "Heavenly Father," he said, "I had faith in you, I prayed to you to save me, and yet you did nothing. Why?" God gave him a puzzled look, and replied "I sent you two boats and a helicopter, what more did you expect?"

Although we often laugh at this story, many people are drowning because they are not using the gifts God gives them with the opportunities He sends to experience help. When we expect God to only move in a way that makes sense to us or the way we want we often miss the ability to achieve the success we are looking for.

Are you ready to experience a limitless world of opportunity that awaits you as an entrepreneur? Do not look at the size of the problem , but focus on the size of your God (and don't box Him in.)

Even though your situation may appear challenging you must remember—the power of Pharoah was no match for the power of God. God has a plan to move you into prosperity, but you must be willing to want what you can not see more than what you see. Remember, the Egyptians at one point said and I paraphrase "Did you bring us out to die, at least in Egypt we knew what to expect?" The path of the entrepreneur is a path of faith and favor through hard work and steadfastness.

When you finally reach that point of being sick and and tired of being sick and tired can you start to believe for the impossible? Are you ready to step out into what you don't know into what God knows?

He will lead you in step with His will as you place your trust in Him and listen to His voice. Let me remind you once again, move with Him, not ahead of Him or behind Him. You do this by committing your plans to Him and He lines up your thoughts with His will. Are you convinced that entrepreneurs are a positive need for the future of our families and the happiness and success God wants for us? Do you believe that becoming an entrepreneur gives you more time and opportunity to bless the lives of others?

This information no doubt has stirred up your desire to express your entrepreneurial abilities, however before you quit your job and jump out into the unknown read the next chapter, "The Path From Employee to Entrepreneur." Yes, Entrepreneurs are the purpose of God for His glory and your success. Don't let your gift sit idle. "BEAT" the odds of becoming a boxed in employee!

B—elieve in your ability
E—ducate yourself
A—ct on your belief
T—ake control of your future

Entrepreneurs make their paycheck
Employees get their paycheck

Entrepreneurs set their schedule
Employees get scheduled

Entrepreneurs plan a vacation
Employees get a vacation

Entrepreneurs have limitless
opportunity
Employees have guidelines

Entrepreneurs depend on God's favor
Employees depend on man's favor

CHAPTER 4

The Path From
Employee to Entrepreneur

By now you probably have a pretty big desire to step out into what God has gifted you with and make a successful career for yourself. For many the big question is, "How do I move from employee to entrepreneur?" It's kind of like receiving a new car, you can't wait to get behind the wheel and start driving. When you see the car in the driveway your natural desire is to drop everything and take off on a road trip. Think what would happen if you left all your daily duties—the laundry, the schooling (if you're a home school mom), the cooking, the cleaning, etc…. Obviously it would be there waiting for you and probably piling up even more. This is similar to what can happen when our excitement to use our new found gift causes us to neglect our present duties. Obviously, if we jump out into entrepreneurship without a solid foundation we will fall. Like the chores piling up, so do the bills, thus hindering us from investing into our gift which is meant to bring success.

We need to ask ourselves, "Where does God need me now, to supply for me?" If we are where God wants us the supply will be sufficient to meet the need, even though it may not be what we desire to be doing. God desires us to work well where we are at on the way to where we are going. This doesn't mean you put your gift on hold, but it does mean you need to balance your gift with your current circumstances. Unfortunately what can happen when we discover our gift (the plan of God for success in our life) we often move out ahead of God setting us farther from the desired destination. This can often lead to discouragement and often takes more faith to keep following. Being an employee while you pursue your gift is not a bad thing. Employment can serve as a form of mentorship, although the ultimate goal is to train on your way to obtaining entrepreneurship. We should be looking at what God may be trying to use our current position to teach us that will profit us when we become an entrepreneur. I can tell you with assurance that God has a reason for where you are to prepare you for where He wants you.

In 2001 I questioned God how losing our home and becoming homeless with five small children could be where He wanted me. Now, I want to say here that we had discovered the gift God wanted to use in our lives toward success but we weren't sure of how to go about getting there. We had confirmation that my husband was to leave the career he had at that time, however we became so focused on the vision that we did lose sight of the present and found ourselves trying to bring our gift to success before it was time. God had spoken to us to go one direction and not convinced that this was a good idea we, like Jonah, went another way. Needless to say, when you go the opposite direction of where you are told to go it doesn't turn out so well and delays your journey. We found ourselves not only homeless, but hungry, broke and unsure of what to do next. God generally doesn't give you the full set of blueprints. He purposely gives you just what you need now to get you moving forward. If He had told the Israelites of the challenges they would face on the way to the Promised Land they might have stayed in Egypt and missed their blessing.

Your gift will produce challenge, however a challenge conquered becomes success. It is only in passive acceptance of our current situation do we accept defeat.

What if you get off course, you may be wondering? What I can tell you is God 's will for our lives never changes even if our course may need redirected.

Don't allow the enemy to discourage you in this time of preparation. We must stay on guard to this mentality that can steal our future. You see the Bible tells us,

"God never changes his mind when he gives gifts or when he calls someone."
Romans 11:29

Let me say also, God will take what was meant for harm (to cause you to give up and quit) and turn it to good.

"Even though you planned evil against me, God planned good to come out of it..."
Genesis 50:20

You see it is the enemies number one goal to cause us to become discouraged especially after God has revealed the gift He has placed within us. If the enemy steals our gift through the position we are at he has the power to kill and destroy our future success. This is why it is crucial to keep traveling steadily toward becoming an entrepreneur and not becoming discouraged on the journey.

"The thief comes to steal, kill and destroy; I came that they might have life and have it more abundantly."
John 10:10

In 2009 I saw how God turned all of the challenges we faced to good for His glory. Through these trials I developed a heart of compassion for the hurting. I realized there were many who had become discouraged in their situations and were victims to circumstances. Ann Haney Ministries was birthed with a mission to help the hurting and see people become not only overcomers, but achievers. I desperately want to see people reach their desired destination and have all God has for them. We do this by working diligently where we are on the way to where God is taking us. Never doubt God's plan for your life. Do not quit before you taste success.

"Be courageous. I have seen many depressions in business. Always America has emerged from these stronger and more prosperous. Be brave as your fathers before you. Have faith! Go forward!" [1]

Thomas Edison

Thomas Edison was no stranger to the challenges of pursuing a dream. His first job was selling candy and newspapers at the railroad. At the age of 12 he held his first profitable job selling his newspaper publication on the train. At the age of 15 he became a telegraph operator. He continued to devote all of his spare time to his inventions. Then in 1869 Edison quit his job to pursue his inventions completely.

66

[1] http://www.brainyquote.com/quotes/authors/t/thomas_a_edison.html

After finding out the world was not ready for his invention (the electronic vote machine) he went to work at Western Union. However, more of his time was spent focusing on his gift than his job and he went broke and moved to New York where he was homeless and slept in the basement of a building until he received a break and was hired as a repair man. This time Edison worked on his inventions while diligently doing his job. This paid off as he was paid for his invention $40,000 which began his road to success.[1]

"Many of life's failures are people who did not realize how close they were to success when they gave up."[2]

Thomas Edison

The truth is you never really know when things will drastically change for you. The importance is not forgetting the truth of where you are at and working towards where you are going.

Remember the story of Joseph (Gen. 37-41) how his excitement about his dream caused him to gain the disfavor of his family and landed him in some rough circumstances (which is also an important point—be careful who you share your dream with). Thomas Edison also did this in his life when he partnered up with a man who sold an invention he worked on keeping all the proceeds for himself and none for Edison. When we look at the life of Joseph we see his circumstances did change when he became second in command of Egypt.

[1]http://inventors.about.com/cs/inventorsalphabet/a/electricity_5.htm
[2])http://www.brainyquote.com/quotes/authors/t/thomas_a_edison.html

Joseph endured much challenge on the way to the fulfillment of his dream and God's plan for his life. However, through his life we can see God directed each of his steps giving him favor where he was on the way to where He was taking him. Joseph worked 13 years until his dream came into a successful reality.

I do not believe God puts the same time table on every individual regarding the successfulness of their gift. Through this book my hope is to show you some of the pitfalls we can avoid and the lives we can learn from to make decisions that will lead us in an expedient way to our goal.

Your goal will become a reality when your desire to benefit others with your gift becomes more important to you than the benefits you will receive. This is when the success of the gift becomes evident in your life.

"I never perfected an invention that I did not think about in terms of the service it might give others..."
Thomas Edison

When you desire to put the needs of others before your own you have discovered the key to being "chosen" by God for successfulness.

"So the last shall be first, and the first last: for many are called, but few chosen."
Matthew 20:16

What is being said here is this—we all have a call and a gift to exercise this call, however few will grasp the true concept that leads to success. When our heart, character and attitude are properly aligned (wishing to bless others through our career before ourselves, then our career will serve as a greater blessing to our lives.) Be careful in your thinking here. Many will try and convince you that you need to show them favoritism and some even pity. Some people will try and use this to mean we should give all we have without regard to our own financial stability. This is not what Christ is saying here. He looks upon the heart. He knows why you do what you do and what you are thinking.

Now that we understand some of the mentalities that need to be in alignment for the success of our gift, what do we go next?

So what should I do now to prepare for entre-preneurship?

Let me answer this by breaking down the following scripture. I believe this will give us a lot of insight into wise business management,

*She **considers** a [new] field before she buys or **accepts** it, [**expanding** prudently and not courting neglect of her present duties by assuming other duties]; with her savings she **plants** fruitful vines in her vineyards."*
Proverbs 31:16

In other words don't quit your day job. Expanding prudently not courting neglect of your other duties basically means add to your life carefully and sensibly without stopping what you are already doing. Does this mean you will always be adding more and never changing your journey? Not at all! However, there are stages of planting (progress) that must take place to achieve fruitful (successful) vineyards (businesses).

Think about a young child for a moment. Curiosity is usually the drive behind their first steps. They see something they want and try to figure out how to reach it. But, when is the last time you saw a baby jump out of the crib into a full sprint to get the toy at the other end of the room. A child does not know everything they need to know about crawling, climbing, walking or running. Their success is driven by their desire, but their desire can only be reached in stages. A baby will start with crawling movements to get closer to the desired toy. Through their frustrations to reach it quicker they will learn to walk and even run. However, even in these stages the child can reach a dilemma when they get to the toy, but it is out of reach. Is this the end to the attempt? Although, the child may let out a frustrated scream to try and get someone else to give them their desire they will quickly learn that it can be accomplished faster when they learn to climb. We can learn a lot from the determination of a baby. We should be driven by our curiosity to reach our goal in a timely manner. Then when the goal seems so close, but still not quite close enough to grasp, we climb. Granted we may let out a frustrat-

-ed scream or two and even look to man to help us reach it faster. But, ultimately the success lies within our desire to learn. If we continually look for the easy answer we will find a limited success with no knowledge of how to conquer our next business challenge.

Stages of Preparation for Full Time Entrepreneurship:

1. Considering Your Business
2. Accepting Your Business
3. Expanding Your Business While Employed
4. Reinvesting (planting) In Business

Let's look at Proverbs 31:16 (which by the way is a principle that applies to everyone) in more detail for the purpose of achieving success in business.

STEP 1: CONSIDERING YOUR BUSINESS

We are to carefully consider the new trade (field) we are thinking of pursuing. There are several things we must do in these beginning stages.

#1— Obtain knowledge about the field

Read up on the area you are pursuing. Use the internet, books, people who work in that field, statistics, articles ,media, periodicals or anything else that might give insight into the pros and cons that have been encountered past and present. Knowledge is the protector of your life, keeping you from venturing where it isn't wise.

"...and the advantage of knowledge is that wisdom preserves the life of him who has it"

Ecclesiastes 7:12

You see when you learn all you can about what you are planning to pursue, you will be full aware what is and is not in your best interest to do. We are to carefully consider the new trade (field) we are thinking of pursuing.

#2 Prepare a Business Overview

This is where the importance of a business plan overview comes into effect. This will not be your final business plan; you are only in the considering stages at this point. However, when considering starting a business many things need to be thought about. Most of the time we do not retain all of the great ideas or intentions we have for our business unless we write them down. Writing these down will help you to organize a well-prepared Final Business Plan once you have decided to accept this field. If you are jointly doing this with your spouse it is important to discuss the details of expectations you both have regarding your business. Many times the purpose of entrepreneurship is to bring one or both partners home from the workplace. It is important that each partner agrees on their part in making this a reality. Generally, the workload will increase on both in an effort to achieve a greater end result in a timely manner. All successful entrepreneurs will tell you it took more effort to get there, but it was worth the work to receive the freedom.

I often ask people in my couponing presentations "if it took you 6 weeks of committed effort to reduce your grocery bill by 50%, would it be worth it?" Most all say, "absolutely!" You see the point, it will take a certain amount of effort to get where you are going, but it will be worth it in the end.

What if both partners aren't 100% committed to the goal. You might be thinking, "My spouse doesn't see the potential blessing I see yet, is it still possible to make this a reality?" I want to assure you it is. It is true that God sees us as one and it is important for us to be in unity regarding our futures, but it is God's job to do the convincing not ours. Should we still pursue the use of our gifts to build success? Yes, however, don't let your steadfastness be based on your spouses reactions to your call. Doing this sets you up for disappointment and sets up your spouse for failure to feel important to you. Now I want to clear up any misconceptions you might have about this. I am not saying do what you want with no regard to your spouses wishes, but what I am saying is this—God places individual calls on each of us as He desires that is not dependent on man's wishes. God will bring together you and your spouse in one accord in His way and His timing. Our job is to be diligent with the gift He has given us.

We read in Luke 1 that Joseph planed to divorce Mary quietly because he wasn't quite sold on the call upon her life. It took an appearance from the angel of the Lord to convince him (not her). Fortunately Joseph immediately believed and moved in unity with Mary on the call upon their lives.

However, also in Luke 1 we see that Zachariah's response to the call was not one of immediate belief when the angel of the Lord appeared to him. He was old, had believed for years and had grown to a state of settling. Because of his disbelief God punished him, not allowing him to speak until the birth of the promise. Many times men often grow weary, especially in middle age, as their lives seem to be less than they've expected (This can happen to women as well.) This often makes it hard for them to believe God for great future endeavors. However, notice the promised gift was birthed for the intended purpose and Zachariah's disbelief did not stop this. Do not discourage if your spouse is not yet on board with what God has spoken to you regarding your gift. God knows what it will take to bring about their belief. In Zachariah's case he was silenced, only to watch the plan unfold. Only God knows what your spouse needs to believe and this He will do to cause your gifts to be used for His glory.

Now let's take a look at the components that should be included in this Business Overview:

The Mission Statement
Time Investment
Money Investment For Start-Up
Competition
Sole Proprietorship or Partnership
Charity Support
Geographical Marketing
Promotional Marketing
Projected Goal

Each of these are important in determining if this field is something to venture into. These will serve as a guideline. Remember, you are still in step 1- Considering Your Business.

The Mission Statement
(this should be why you are doing what you're doing and your goal in doing it)

*It is important that you give God credit for your business endeavor. Remember, if we want to be successful He must be the key factor in why we are doing what we are doing and you must be willing to let other people know this. (Christ says, "Whoever is ashamed of me and my words, I will also be ashamed of him before my Father." Mark 8:38) I would suggest incorporating a key scripture that sums up the purpose of your business. Don't forget to include the name of your business here.

The following is an example:
Business Foundation—*Helping Others Grow Their Advertising Outreach Regardless of Size*

Example Slogan: *Equal Service to All!*

Example Scripture: *"To show no prejudice or partiality....James 2:1*

Example Mission Statement: *John Doe Graphics is committed to providing equal and exceptional service to all clients with the sole purpose of providing them complete, convenient, and quality service with a special regard to customer satisfaction.*

How much TIME can I personally invest into my business?

Evaluate your current obligations and determine the amount of time you can set aside to pursue and perfect your business WITHOUT taking away from other duties. This is a very important question to answer realistically. If a plan is going to be success- ful it will need to be realistic. If it is not you will find yourself discouraged and often quitting before you get off to a good start.

"Look carefully then how you walk, not as unwise but as wise, making the best use of the time .."
Ephesians 5:15

Try every night to spend at least 1-2 hours on busi- ness preparation and an 8 hour day on your day off. Try and leave one day a week for rest (usually Sun- day) when no work is to be done. If you commit yourself to this you will be amazed at how quickly you will progress toward your full time business as an entrepreneur. You may have to adjust this if your schedule is more than a 40 hour week, how- ever, if it is less you should be able to devote a sig- nificantly larger amount of time towards the growth of your business. The growing stages are more time consuming, but the effort will pay off if you stay committed. Balance is the key!

"So let's not allow ourselves to grow fatigued doing good At the right time we will harvest a good crop if we don't give up, or quit.
Galatians 6:9

How much MONEY can I personally invest into my business?

A key factor to include in your overview is a realistic idea of what you can personally invest in your business. This will require you to have budget in place with an amount set aside for the purpose of business growth. There are many ways we can be wise investors and cut our household expenses. One of my most popular ways is taught through couponing. My family cut our grocery expenses by $800 a month by spending only 1 hour a week. Would $800 a month be beneficial in helping you grow your business? It not only helped with our business finances but, increased our food supply. (See my website for more on these presentations entitled— Changing Your Life Through Couponing) Your goal needs to be using what you have wisely to grow more. You don't have to start with a lot of money to build a lot of money. Let me tell you about my first business venture in 2001. I had designed a planner to keep all my children's records neatly within one book. This planner, known as "The Homeschool Daily Planner For Curriculum" (later became a 5 year running best seller), was created on my home computer. I took it to a copy/print store to produce a copy to submit to potential buyers. My first copy was produced at a non-profitable cost. However, I stepped out in faith, knowing I had a niche product, and submitted to a major online store. After a year of continual submittals my book was accepted. Now you have to remember-I didn't have any way of producing these other than my home computer, so my anxious concern was, "what if they order 1,000 copies?" Well, they didn't. They ordered 10, which I could produce sufficiently. As each order grew I was able to invest in a table top copier and eventually to a large office duplexing copier. A funny fact I want to mention here is when God is in your gift He even extends the life of your copier. His call never lacks His supply. Our little table top copier produced over 1 million copies and had a good life. The point I want to make to you in this story is this— Don't let lack of finances control your pursuit of success! It is important to mention that many grants are available for start-up businesses, business women, non-profit organizations and more. The resources are readily available and should be used to benefit your business.

"My people perish from lack of knowledge..."
Hosea 4:6

NOT LACK OF RESOURCES!

Do remember, what you can invest is still important to determine. We knew what we had before we started and made our plan on faith and facts. Stepping out in faith is not an opportunity to be foolish. Look at the facts of what you are trying to accomplish and what it will cost you to do it.

"Is there anyone here who, planning to build a new house, doesn't first sit down and figure the cost so you'll know if you can complete it? If you only get the foundation laid and then run out of money, you're going to look pretty foolish."
Luke 14:28-29

It will be necessary to make investments to get your business off the ground. You should set aside out of your weekly income, if you hold another job, to further the growth of your business until it is bringing in its own source of revenue. As the business takes off I would suggest putting everything it brings in back into the business to speed the growth of it.

This may not always be possible, especially if you are depending on the income to supplement your current paycheck. In this case you will need to pay yourself as an employee of the business. Talk to an accountant as to how to go about this in proper business legality. You will not want to use all of your profits of the business to live on or you will quickly find yourself in financial trouble and inability to grow your business. Think about the repair that needs to be made to office equipment or the order that comes in for a depleted product supply. Gradual growth is better than no growth. What is acquired at a gradual pace will usually develop into continual wealth. Do you remember the story of Bezalel in the Bible? God filled him with the gift of skill, ability and know how for making all sorts of things. God commanded the people to go to work building the Tent of Meeting for worship. The offerings to complete the work kept coming in so that more than enough was collected. (Exodus 36)

"There was plenty of material for all the work to be done. Enough and more than enough."
Genesis 36:7

Let me assure you that what you have is enough to complete the work God has for you through the gift He has given you. God's plan is for you to use your gift to accomplish a purpose and money is not an obstacle for Him to bring this about. God will always give you enough to get you where He needs you even if it's not sufficient in your eyes.

Common Start-Up Expenses:

Administrative Costs—Business License, Permits, Insurance, Office Supplies, Product Packaging, Shipping and Postage

Technology Costs—Office Equipment (computer, Printer, Copier, Software, Security, Internet, Phone, Website)

Professional Costs—Copyrights, Patents, Accountant, Trademark, Consultation, Bank Account

Item/Product Costs—Materials for Production, Parts, Product Packaging

Marketing Costs—Vendor Fairs, Social Media, Brochures, Flyers, Public Relations (Media Coverage), Advertising

Start up expenses will vary based upon the type of business you plan on going into. Some will require more start up expense then others, but remember if God planned for these expenses and knows what you need to get going. Look for the areas of start up income He opens up to you. Many times grants or obtainable side jobs will reveal themselves that will provide for the immediate need. Don't limit your ability by the size of your bank account.

<u>Who are the competitors to my business?</u>

Let me say first off, if God has gifted you to do this it will be successful despite the competition. However, it is important to know what others are doing for the purpose of marketing your business. By knowing the strategies they use you can look for a unique way to market your business that the competition might not be doing. Here is where your innovator mindset comes into use. Building off the positives of what someone else is doing, but adding your own unique touch to create something a little different. All successful businesses will be aware of how their competition conducts business. Let's say for example a competitor company offers a great service but lack good customer relations. This would be where you want to target your business. While offering the same service, you now offer something they don't-good customer service.. Which by the way, is crucial to all successful businesses. Now, obviously you are not going to make everyone happy all the time, but a dissatisfied customer will market your business negatively. Always do what you can to please the customer even if it means you take a loss on one every now and then.

<u>Sole Proprietorship or Partnership</u>

Sole Proprietorship—owned and operated by one person

Partnership—2 or more agree to share ownership and management

A sole proprietorship is generally the cheapest and easiest business to establish. Most start-up companies choose this form of business. However, the responsibility is great upon the owner as he assumes responsibility for all losses as well as the profits. Most sole proprietorships will require a business license and in some cases a business tax. Each state may vary on the exact regulations on this. A sole proprietor is responsible for all business debt and this liability could extend to personal assets. Try to run your business as efficiently as possible as to not incur debt.

A partnership has advantages as well as disadvantages. In a partnership each partner has gifts they bring to the table for the success of the company. This can increase the potential opportunities for the business and can equalize the workload. One disadvantage might be the fact that each is responsible for any business debt and long-term financing is dependent upon each partner's personal assets. A contract needs to be established if entering into a partnership. Whether you are good friends or not is not the issue here. This is necessary to protect both parties from misunderstandings and keep each one accountable to the other. This should be looked upon as a safety net for both, not a restraining agreement. Many friendships have been ruined by business deals gone bad. A good potential partner should be more than willing to sign a contract as a form of protecting their friendship.

Charity Support

All businesses that desire to be successful know this one principle—*If you want to be successful you must give away some of your profits.*

This is a must for all businesses! Determine what charity or charities you wish to support with some of your profits. This principle is a scriptural principle that brings abundance into a business. After all, it only makes sense that we should give since the world was founded on the love of God given to us.

"Give, and you will receive. Your gift will return to you in full--pressed down, shaken together to make room for more, running over, and poured into your lap. The amount you give will determine the amount you get back."
Luke 6:38

Notice the amount you give will determine the amount you get back. In business there will be times you need to just choose to bless someone as God leads you, even on top of your regular charity support. When you do this God opens up opportunities that you never expected. These opportunities become a blessing for your business and an opportunity for God to receive glory. Always remember to give praise where praise is due. Thank God for His continued provision.

Geographical Marketing

It is important to also include within your Overview

the geographical area where your product or service will be most likely to succeed. For example, if you have a great new product for snow skiers you probably want to market to states where skiing is a frequent sport. Some products and services will be universal, however some are more region specific and more profit will be achieved by marketing them in those areas. Do your research and see where your product will flourish the most.

Promotional Marketing

Decide what types of marketing you plan on doing with your product or service. This can be anything from Flyers/Brochures to Social Media. I will discuss all the various types of marketing in chapter 7.

Projected Goal

Finally, the last component of your Overview should be your projected goal for your business. What do you hope to achieve by offering your product pertaining to the customer? What do you hope to achieve by offering your product as the CEO of your business? What are your short term goals? What are your long term goals? What is your plan of steps to accomplish this goal?

STEP 2: ACCEPTING YOUR BUSINESS

Upon completing your Business Overview you should have a pretty good idea of what your business is going to involve and you are ready to include the next steps in accepting your business. At this point you will have an idea of what the cost and commitment of your business will be.

#1—THE FINAL BUSINESS PLAN

This will serve as your summarized plan for submittal to investors or anyone else in regards to helping fund your business. However, it is always best to start slow with what you have as opposed to borrowing money. Debt free building will profit your business more in the long run.

"...and the borrower is slave to the lender"
Prov. 22:7

Marketing Analysis
Target Market—(This could be age/geographical/ married or single/ etc…)

*A target market is who you are trying to reach with your product or service

Sales Potential— (How many are currently using this type of product or similar product or service. What is the demand?)

Marketing Potential— (How able are you to reach your target market? What marketing tactics will you be able to realistically do?)

Marketing Strategy—(What niche do you have that competitor's might not? What are potential customers interested in that others don't have?)

Pricing— (Research the competition, however be sure you can profit from the price you set. I believe in setting a consistent retail price to all potential retailers with a contract that the item is not to be sold for less. Why? Because many larger companies will under sale the entrepreneurs if given the chance and most people will buy where an item is cheapest. We are in business to make money and cannot compete with the larger companies if we don't require a set price. It's your item/service—you set the price)

I actually experienced this situation through an early mistake in my own business. I allowed the interested retailer a greater discount than I had given others and was selling my own product for on my website. Why did I do this? I wanted their business, however quickly learned that they would have negotiated with me because I had contracts with their competitors. A little too late, but lesson learned. This later cost my business more when I attended a vendor fair and had to lower the cost of my book to meet what they were selling it for at a nearby booth. Stay in business, price smart!

Distribution—(Where do you plan to promote your product or service? Investors will want to know the likeliness of success for your plan of distribution.)

Competition Analysis—(How much competition do you have? What is the success of your competition? How long has your competition been in business? How close is the competition geographically?)

Product Development— (What are the costs associated with producing the product? These are all of your production costs including shipping supplies, postage, packaging, etc...)

Cash Flow of Business— (Costs, Profits, Labor, Overhead, Taxes. Any expenses or profits associated with the business. Investors are generally interested in a net cash flow statement showing the net profit of the business.)

Estimated Return on Investment—(This is your projected goal of ability to repay investments. Again, this may not be necessary, there are many grants available to business women, business owners, start up businesses, etc… I would be sure and check all these out prior to getting an investor.)

#2—MENTORSHIP

Obtaining a mentor is a very important part to establishing a successful business. Mentors can come in many areas, but all serve one main goal and that is to help their student/client to achieve business success. Let's take a look at some of the types of mentors we find helpful with our businesses.

Career Coaches— Are a wise investment for the new entrepreneur, the developing entrepreneur, and the expanding entrepreneur. Career coaches serve as a mentor who helps you get your ideas in action from start to finish. They offer a wealth of knowledge taking you from confusion to completion. st career coaches offer a variety of services to their clients, from online, phone and in person possibilities. Their fees are based upon your needs for their particular services.

Business Owners—They serve as a great tool to the hands on experience you may need. Contacting a business owner you may know and getting some advice on the functionality of the business is a great way to get your feet wet before you take on your own.

Other Successful Entrepreneurs—These can be friends, pastors, acquaintances, etc.. Some of these may be in your field of interest which would serve as a great person to learn from. Often they will have obtained a large amount of knowledge on how to use their gift to produce substantial income in a field you are pursuing.

As I mentioned earlier, my son trained under the mentorship of our pastor and a close friend in film making. This gave him extra knowledge he needed and an edge on the market. He trained for several years and continues to train to increase his learning and opportunity potential.

Regarding mentors, they hold the key to achieving a more expedient path to success for the entrepreneur. The more you learn from them, the more you will be able to teach others.

"Without consultation, plans are frustrated, but with many counselors they succeed. "
Proverbs 15:22

STEP 3: EXPANDING YOUR BUSINESS WITH WORK AND HOME

This is the part where we are balancing our time with work. This is probably the hardest part of any of the four key ingredients. With expansion comes more duty and more discipline. Usually this time frame will affect everyone who is in your life. How you manage during the expansion process will determine how successfully your business grows. One thing I have discovered is we must be willing to expand slower than we like and be more committed than we often want to. It is not an option to put aside our other obligations to speed up our goal. You remember Thomas Edison.

"There's an opportune time to do things, a right time for everything on the earth…"
Ecclesiastes 3:1

There are several key ways we expand our business in a balanced manner to receive the greatest result. We do not want to neglect any of these ingredients as they are a key to happy and successful businesses. Successful Businesses do not make happy businesses. We can be successful and still be miserable. Our end goal is to produce a successful business that brings enjoyment to our lives.

I can tell you from experience, although human reasoning says you will have more time if you leave some of these out, it is not true. I speak from experience. Miracles transpire where human reasoning leaves off.

IMPORTANT DUTIES OF A HOUSEHOLD

#1—SET ASIDE TIME FOR DAILY DEVOTIONS

I recommend doing this at the start of the day. Doing so will refresh you mentally. You'll find yourself better equipped to calmly handle the stresses of the day. It will provide you with a positive outlook that is catchy (Kindness is catchy.) Think about it for a minute— how often has a small problem turned into a gigantic problem when you were quick to react. Did it take a lot of time to sort out the rights and wrongs, the apologies and fresh starts? What could have been handled differently and cost only 5 minutes has now become a 2 hour problem. Understand? A right refreshed mind saves time and energy and allows you to move on to other things (pursuing your gift.)

#2—SET ASIDE FAMILY TIME

This means you will have to establish a set time to call it "quitting time." If you do not do this you will develop burnout, your family will resent your business before you ever get it to the point of benefits. This will mean not bringing work home with you as well. The future successes of the business won't mean much if you don't have anyone to share it with. This will be hard because we have tendencies to be workaholics. If we can't get where we are going with the ones God has placed in our lives we might need to reevaluate where we are going.

Family time will fill the need for acceptance as well as provide a sense of security. Children will especially feel the love and peace within the home when this principle is kept in place. We must remember the need for acceptance is human instinct. If we do not provide it in the home between parents and children and husband and wife we give a foothold to the enemy to breakdown relationships.

#3—TAKE TIME FOR YOURSELF DAILY

Everyone must have a little "me" time. Be balanced with your me time. If you spend an hour in the bath and then plan on taking your "me" time on top of this you will probably not have time for anyone or anything else. Evaluate how you are spending your time and determine to set aside a specific amount of time to unwind daily. Read, take a bath, get your nails done, go out for coffee, etc… This time will remind you of your value as a person and help your hard work seem worth the effort.

#4—WEEKLY DATE NIGHT WITH SPOUSE

Providing your married this is crucial to the health of the marriage. Even if your funds for a night out are limited, be creative. A drive in the country, a cup of coffee, home movie and kids to grandma, etc… This is how we show appreciation to our spouse and let them know we have time for them. If our business keeps us from spending time with our spouse it won't be long and our spouse will develop their own evaluation of their importance to us. Strong Marriages require solid commitments.

#5—DELEGATING DUTIES OF THE BUSINESS

Incorporate your children into the functions of your business. I have found that even the youngest child can do something to help. It might be having them learn a chore of an older child (taught by the older child) so you can delegate a business task to the older one. Teaching your children early to work for the business is a form of mentoring. This will give them a satisfaction of responsibility and trust and confidence that they are capable of success. As it is possible give them opportunities to earn money for jobs completed to give them a drive for entrepreneurship. You would be surprised what all ages of children can do when given the chance. Allow them the chance to succeed, embrace them through failure, and encourage them to try again. After all, we are also in a process of learning and if we weren't allowed to try again, where would we be? Remember your most important audience is your child!

Let me share with a story from personal experience actually regarding the writing of this book. Being a home school mother my first obligation is to my children, however I knew time was winding down and I could not seem to accomplish this project. I made the mistake of thinking if I allowed my children a week vacation (to be taken early for Spring break) I could accomplish this task. My first mistake was neglecting my first duty. I found that nothing was accomplished that week and my frustration was high as I was left with this dilemma. God drew my attention to David in 1 Samuel 17:20:

"So David rose up early next morning, LEFT THE SHEEP WITH A KEEPER… and went as he was commanded."

Notice that when a task needed done, his regular duties were covered by someone else instead of neglected. When we take on more it is not a free pass to neglecting other things but rather an opportunity for delegating tasks to others. So my new plan of action was to have my mother substitute teach for a week to allow the completion of this book. As you guessed, the book was completed and my other duties were also. I thank the Lord for wonderful mothers. Just a note here for parents—including your children in building your business is an investment in their lives not an unpaid chore with no future reward. Teach them business skills by allowing them to actively be involved in the business. This not only gives them opportunity for future advancement but, lightens you load.

STEP 4: INVESTING IN YOUR BUSINESS

#1—CREATING MULTIPLE CASH FLOW

We have talked about investing a little bit at the beginning of this chapter, however I want to take a look at a different aspect of investing in this part. What we notice in this part of Prov. 31:16 is that she takes the savings (money she saves from the field she expands) and plants it in something that will bring growth. Her prudence allows her to reinvest in something that will produce more fruit.

"….with money she sets aside she plants fruitful vines in her vineyard."

Prudent expansion allows for increase. This is where we are to use our business to branch out in different directions. Have you ever heard the saying, "don't put all your eggs in one basket?" Why do you suppose that is? The reason we are to plant in different places is because variety creates stability. All businesses will experience slow seasons, however if your business has a variety of services or products the stability of your business will be more secure. Looking into further depth of Proverbs 31, you will notice this woman does many things to supply income for her family. She trades, designs, sells, and is a woman of skill who properly understands the importance of investing, sales, and marketing.

Let me explain what I mean. Let's say lawn care business is the trade you have chosen. Now this one is fairly obvious—there will be times when the need is not there during the winter months. How then can you use this gift to expand and still create stable income? Possibly offering other services like tree trimming, landscaping, hanging Christmas lights, cleaning gutters, etc…

Do you get the idea? Obviously you could choose several areas to invest in, even if they are not related as shown in this scripture. The importance is not what you choose, but rather that you choose according to the gifts God has given you. God does not usually limit individuals to only one gift. The gifts God gives you will generally enhance each other. Running several businesses is common amongst entrepreneurs.

Are you ready to take on something new and experience the freedom and success that awaits you? Energy is defined as an initiative and ambitious readiness to undertake new projects. So what is your energy level? Can you envision becoming an successful entrepreneur? Set your vision towards the goal and do not look to the left or the right. When your eyes wander, so does your heart, costing you to lose focus. The time to focus harder is when the energy you are exerting is greater then the results you are seeing. This is when we are most often tempted to look for another way. Stay focused and arrive successfully!

"Where there is no vision, the people perish.."
Proverbs 29:18

The Message Bible says it this way—

"If people can't see what God is doing, they stumble all over themselves; but when they attend to what He reveals they are most blessed."
Proverbs 29:18

Doesn't this describe our mentalities so often? When we can't see what God is doing when we are worn out, we finding ourselves in places we aren't meant to be, losing sight of why we started out in the first place. Your thoughts and your actions are both crucial to keeping your vision alive and becoming a successful entrepreneur.

"The thoughts of the steadily diligent tend only to plenteousness, but everyone who is hasty only to want."
Proverbs 21:5

In other words—line up your thoughts with your actions and you will achieve abundance; no doubt about it. Steer clear of thinking one thing and acting on something else. If there is no agreement within yourself there can be no success.

Are you convinced that entrepreneurs are a positive need for the future of our families and the happiness and success God wants for us? Do you believe that becoming an entrepreneur gives you more time and opportunity to bless the lives of others? Yes, Entrepreneurs are the purpose of God for His glory and your success.!

Establishing a business is no easy task. Most all businesses take approximately two years to become well established. Therefore, if you want to eat while you are building your business stay employed and work diligently in your free time to secure a good foundation for your business. Remember, Thomas Edison learned to balance by working in areas of interest gaining knowledge, while in his free time he grew his gift by practicing it until he perfected it. His life was a life of trial and error we can learn a lot from. Eventually his work gave him the creditability to be an independent success on his own. Balancing work with your gift is important. Too much work leaves no time for growing your gift and too much gift growing will leave you hungry.

Anything that will drastically change your life is worth the time and effort it takes to give it a solid foundation. Moving at your desired speed does not always give success to your business. Only when we move at God's will we achieve the successfulness we are hoping for.

In closing, keep on traveling toward becoming an entrepreneur while you are still an employee by lining up your thoughts with your actions.

"Jesus said, "No procrastination. No backward looks. You can't put God's kingdom off till tomorrow. Seize the day."
Luke 9:62

Set your focus

Defy discouragement

Empower your mind

Equip your hands

Set your feet to motion

CHAPTER 5

The Opposition
To Your
Gift

Why is it that some become conquerors and successful entrepreneurs and others don't? What factors play a negative role into hindering our ability to succeed and experience all God has for us? In this chapter I want to look at several components that keep us from where God wants us to be.

Some of the contributing factors are as follows:

Length of Financial Struggle
Impatience
Negative Thinking
Fear of Failure
Jealousy
Human Reasoning
Unsupportive People

Let's look at each of these in detail.

#1 Length of Financial Struggle—-

Do you ever feel like you are working harder and getting no where, only to be expected to produce more effort? It seems the moment something positive happens a negative is just around the corner waiting to discourage you. I have been there. One minute you are on an emotional high with a glimmer of hope for what God might be doing and the next minute the hope is faded out by the problems that invade. The car develops a knock, the ice maker quits working, the kids inform you they've outgrown their shoes, and the cat's out of food. All of this when you just thought things were looking up.

Let's take a look into the lives of the Israelites in Exodus 6:8-9. They had experienced hard, cruel labor by the Pharoah for 400 years. They had finally come to a point when they just said, "It is what it is", and settled for their bondage. Then God sends Moses with a glimmer of hope informing them of God's plan to take away all this slavery to the jobs they had been confined to for all these years. Did they see this glimmer of hope? Unfortunately not, Exodus 6:9 tells us,

"Moses told this to the Israelites , but they refused to listen to Moses because of their impatience and anguish of spirit and because of their cruel bond-age."

You see this is what happens to us many times. We have been in the situation so long we fail to believe. God never works miracles through disbelief.

"Then Jesus answered her, "O woman, great is your faith! Be it done for you as you desire." And her daughter was healed instantly."
Matthew 15:28

You may wonder why God doesn't do things at a quicker pace or with less struggle to our lives. Honestly, if we had no challenge would we see how much we need Him? In order to reach success we must have faith and faith is needed more when we are in the midst of the trial This is when God often shows His power. Our faith is an instrument to someone else's ability to succeed. Charles Wesley once said,

"Faith, mighty faith, the promise sees, And looks to God alone; Laughs at impossibilities, And cries it shall be done." [1]

When life is at it's hardest our faith needs to be at it's strongest, claiming God is bigger than my doubt!

"The father instantly cried out, "I do believe, but help me overcome my unbelief!"
Mark 9:24

This assures us we can overcome our doubt and receive the answer to our prayer as this father did. You see back to the Israelites, God reassures His promise again that he will rescue and bring them out with vigorous and special action. He gives His pledge of changeless omnipotence and faithfulness. In other words God is going to use forceful and energetic action that is unexpected through unlimited power in a steadfast course of action. God is on the scene in your situation and will deliver you out of bondage as well.

#2 Impatience—

This opposition hits all of us at one time or another. Abraham was hit with impatience when he got tired of waiting for the gift and took matters into his own hands. I am sure hind sight told Abraham his life would have been a whole lot easier if he had waited for God to move. Instead Abraham conceived a child with Hagaar thinking that maybe this would be how God would give him the descendants he was promised. Do we sometimes try and help God out to speed up the process? When we do this we create more trouble for ourselves than we were meant to have. Moving with God, not ahead of Him is the only way to achieve the success we are hoping for without creating a lot of problems for ourselves on the way. Remember, the scripture about commit our plans unto the Lord? Obviously Abraham did not consult God on this or God would have made his thoughts line up with His plan. God's timing is the only timing that will produce success.

#3 Negative Thinking—

Many are living with this hindrance to their gift. They go from one extreme to the other listening to the lies of the enemy. One minute they are confident the next minute they are defeated. They start to believe the lies of the enemy— "You are not worthy of God's blessing," "You deserve more than God is allowing you to have," "You're going to embarrass yourself," "You're not qualified," "Your product/idea isn't good enough," and the list goes on and on.

Why do we see so many people believing these lies? Most of the time this stems from something in their past that made them feel insignificant and rejected. Rejection will destroy your ability to succeed if you let it get a grip on you. The truth is—it only matters what God says about you. Love Him, live for Him, and He will lead you out of bondage and into success. Where negativity is allowed to grow dreams are destroyed. You see you can and will achieve success in your life if you remove disbelief. It is not your strength that will accomplish success, but God's strength through your surrendered life.

"I can do ALL things through Christ who strengthens me."
Philippians 4:13

Notice it doesn't say "some" things. God desires to bring your gift to the surface, but you must defeat the lies of the enemy by claiming your ability through Christ to accomplish all God has for you.

#4 Fear of Failure—–

Now this we can all identify with as one of the enemies favorite weapons. Actually fear is also a form of personal bondage that can stem from our past. However, fear is usually the first thing that attacks us when we step out in a new direction, especially in a direction that leads towards our success. You have heard that fear is false evidence appearing real. How many times do we worry ourselves sick over something that works out for good in the end.? "How are we going fund this product?" "How will I gain creditability when everyone else is already established?" "There's already enough of this out there, how can my idea/product be successful?"

The only fear we are to have is a reverential fear of the Lord. When we acknowledge the power of God to work in our lives it defeats fear and leads us to riches.

"True humility and fear of the Lord lead to riches, honor, and long life."
Proverbs 22:4

Our future does not lie in what everyone else is doing or the size of our investment. Our individual gifts are meant for success no matter what anyone else does. Do not let fear rob you of a successful future.

#5 Jealousy—-

Jealousy will always keep us from accomplishing our full potential. If we are putting the goal of our success on the desire to be like others we will never reach the goal. God may use you in areas like someone else, but He will never base your life off of someone else's. If you spend to much time wishing to have what someone else has (fame, knowledge, ability, etc...) or wishing to be like someone else you will never see what you can be or were meant to be. It is sad to think many spend their whole life longing for what others have and resenting them for it. In fact the sad truth is many had the ability to have more, but never got past their jealousy to achieve it.

"When we are more concerned about what others are doing, we never see what we could have done."

How can we deal with the frustrations we have when we see other's prosperity when ours is lacking?

"Make a careful exploration of who you are and the work you have been given, and then sink yourself into that. Don't be impressed with yourself. Don't compare yourself to others. Each of you must take responsibility for doing the creative best you can with your own life."
Galatians 6:4-5

That pretty well pins it down. Examine your life and focus on your career. Be humble with no comparison of others, doing your very best with your own ability to be creative.

#6 Human Reasoning—-

Reasoning refers to a logical explanation. I have dis covered that sometimes we are so logical that we cannot see the simplest of things. What doesn't make sense will often be the very thing that delivers the success. Is it logical that a 187,000 pound aircraft can take off from the ground and fly through the air to great distances? No, but they do. It started with an idea of the impossible by the Wright Brothers in 1900 who studied the flight of birds and built the impossible which has become the most popular way to travel long distances today. If human reasoning had been in control of their mind they would have never achieved the impossible.

It's interesting to me how we often believe God for everything except our finances. Why is it we feel we must be in control of this one area of our lives? Do we think He is incapable of providing our needs or maybe we don't think He'll give us what we want. Our ability to gain knowledge should never replace our ability to believe for the unexplainable. I often see people who have so much book knowledge they can't comprehend anything unless there is an explanation for it.

God doesn't follow rules
God makes them

God doesn't ask questions
God gives answers

God doesn't follow facts
God gives faith

Being only motivated with head knowledge will cause you to miss success as much as being only motivated with faith knowledge. God has given us minds for wisdom and hearts for faith to balance together to reach success. (Remember the man who drowned waiting in faith for God?) God works through a combination of faith and intelligence.

#7 Unsupportive People—-

Something that will affect us all at some time or another is people who do not believe in what we are doing or think we are doing it wrong. Sometimes people mean well, but let me assure you God usually doesn't tell others what you should be doing before He tells you. They may believe they know what your gift is (and they may even be right), however, God will tell you what your gift is and not just some

-one else. Other times you will have people who see God working in your life and want to tell you what you should be doing with your gift. I had a lady tell me one time, if I did not sell her the presentation materials I used in my teachings that I was not furthering God's gift the way He meant me too. You will often come across these type of people, who are usually motivated out of jealousy. Often you will find people who are critical of your gift and the business you are pursuing and will do their very best to discredit you and prevent you from being successful. I experienced this situation in a business dealing I once had when a woman spoke negatively about me and the business of couponing I was in. However, this woman never would confront me face to face, only condemned me behind my back. Did this affect my ability to succeed? No, God still blessed my business and even prospered it more so when I continued on despite the challenges she gave me. We must choose not to let anyone discourage us from pursuing our calling.

Opposition—something that fights strongly against something else. What is your opposition? What or who is fighting against the call of God for success on your business?

I know for myself it often seems like my biggest opposition is when God has opened up some opportunities and the hope before me seems high. I can see hope of success in a situation but don't know how it will come about. This is usually when the enemy will discourage me with thoughts like, "Are you sure God can use you?"

"Do you really know what you are talking about?", "Is anyone really benefitting from what you are doing?" I have found that if I let this, it has the potential to destroy my ability to prosper. You see what God tells me in these times is this (and He is telling you too)—"It is not you that have the ability, it is Me." If I have committed my work to Him, He is making it successful despite my abilities or lack of. Our defeats and our victories are determined in our mind. What we believe becomes our ability to succeed. However, our belief must be—"God I am nothing without you. My talents, my abilities are not successful unless you are first in importance to me."

Above all, when God is silent continue on with the last assignment He gave you. You see we tend to get on an emotional high of expectation that thrives on new adventurers and our flesh likes to keep this adventurous feeling going. If God is doing something great at every moment in our business we often get discouraged very quickly. It seems our attention span is like that of a child at times. We are looking for our next exciting happening. This is often the point when the enemy desires to break us down because he knows he has a 50/50 chance that we will become discouraged and blame God. If he breaks us at this point our growth will be stationary. Many times we question God as to why He allows Satan to defeat us here if He is stronger. This time of testing shows not only God our commitment but Satan as well. We must remember God restores double to those who overcome the time of testing as He did with Job.

Don't forget, there is work to be done after the assignment comes and until that assignment is completed God doesn't usually send another opportunity. He knows how much we can handle without overwhelming us. When we are faithful to complete what we have been given at each specific time, He will always provide more opportunity to grow.

When the opposition is "FACED" your business is on its way to success!

"See, the LORD your God has given you the land. Go up and take possession of it as the LORD, the God of your fathers, told you. Do not be afraid; do not be discouraged."
Deut. 1:21

AND DO NOT LET ANYONE (including yourself) OR ANYTHING KEEP YOU FROM BECOMING SUCCESSFUL!

F— aith (belief in the unseen)
A—ction (intentions meet production)
C—ommitment (binding to action)
E—ndurance (staying in the fight)
D—iscipline (self-control)

CHAPTER 6

GIVING AFFECTS YOUR RECEIVING

Many times we see people operating in their gift, but they seem to have no power to achieve success. For instance, they are skilled in a specific field like carpentry doing a great job for someone else, but falling short to meet their own individual needs week after week. Why do you suppose this happens? A gift alone will not make someone successful. It is the condition of the heart which motivates the gift that determines it's ability to succeed. If the carpenter goes in day after day doing a skilled job, but only thinking on what he will gain at the end of the day, his work will be in vain. The effectiveness of our gifts is based upon our desire to bless others. You see God said,

"For God so LOVED the world that He GAVE His only son, that whosover believeth on Him shall not perish, but shall have eternal life."
John 3:16

God loved, God gave, we received. If we are to be like Christ we are to operate in these same three functions. We must first love, then give, and we will receive. To operate in our gift for the sole purpose of blessing our lives, was not God's intent and it remains the number one reason people do not achieve success even when they have found their gift. When the benefits of your gift become less important to you than your ministry with your gift you will start to see the success of your gift change. Have you ever noticed that even businesses like the "super giants" we talked about in chapter 3 do some form of charity giving? Successful business owners know that giving plays a major role in a company's ability to succeed. Now I do want to mention for the continued stability of a business the heart of the giver must be a heart for God. I will discuss this more in the last chapter. Let's look at how your attitude toward giving can affect your abundance,

"[Remember] this: he who sows sparingly and grudgingly, will also reap sparingly and grudgingly, and he who sows generously [that blessings may come to someone] will also reap generously and with blessings."
2 Cor. 9:6

Do you want to experience an abundant business? If so it is necessary to give abundantly. If we give the bare minimum, we will get the bare minimum. The next verse states we are to think it over and make up our mind what we will give. God warns us to think it over, why? Because, it directly affects our increase.

"Let each one [give] as he has made up his own mind and purposed in his heart, not reluctantly or sorrowfully or under compulsion, for God loves (He takes pleasure in, prizes above other things, and is unwilling to abandon or to do without) a cheerful (joyous prompt to do it) giver [WHOSE HEART IS IN HIS GIVING]."
2 Cor. 9:7

Notice "whose heart is in his giving." God looks upon the heart to see if you really have a love for others.

116

So if I give to others out of love and a pure heart can I expect God to bless the success of my business? Let's see:

"And God who provides seed for the sower and bread for eating will also PROVIDE AND MULTIPLY your resources for sowing and increase the fruits of your righteousness [which manifests itself in active goodness, kindness and charity]...thus you will be enriched in ALL things and in EVERY way, so that you can be generous, and [your generosity as it is] administered by us will bring forth thanksgiving to God."
2 Cor. 9:10-11

Do you see the connection? God has promised not only provision for you, but multiplication so that your ability to continue giving is increased. It also tells us we will be enriched (derived from the Greek word (ploutizo)—meaning to make wealthy in material possessions, money, and resources.

God's purpose in giving to us is three-fold—so that we will be able to give to others, enjoy the abundance ourselves AND above all so that His name will be glorified. You have already seen two reasons why God gives us abundance, but what about the third, enjoy the abundance ourselves. Many people believe that if you are a wealthy Christian you are misusing the funds God gives you. I do acknowledge some have been guilty of this, however, is it only the non-Christian who is supposed to enjoy the success of their labor? Absolutely not! However, it is sad to say, many wealthy Christian speakers are condemned because they have a comfortable life-style. Why is it that society never questions the rich man or woman (who are not in ministry positions) who have gained wealth and enjoy a comfortable lifestyle? I believe this is just a clear tactic of the enemy to keep the Christian from having everything God has for them. Satan implants lies through others (usually jealous because of their desire to have what someone else has) in an attempt to make them feel guilty for enjoying the blessings God gives them.

"You worked hard and deserve all you've got coming. ENJOY the blessing! REVEL (take delight) in the goodness!"
Psalm 128:2 MESSAGE BIBLE

Yes, we are to enjoy the work of our hands. It is a gift from God.

"Also, every man to whom God has given riches and possessions, and the power to enjoy them and to accept his appointed lot and to rejoice in his toil—this is the gift of God [to him]."
Eccl. 5:19

We are told to give what we have made up our mind to give in 2 Cor. 9:7. This tells me that God let's us decide according to our heart how much we should give (of course this is above the tithe which God requires.) It is God's will that we be generous givers but not poor Christians. Often in business we can become too greedy or too giving. There is a perfect balance. If we over give we can find our-

-selves in want and often hinder the work God is trying to do in someone else's life. You see when people are in hurting positions they often can't see their way out and too much help can leave them with a dependency on man never discovering the gift God gave them for their own lives. However, under giving can cause us to miss the opportunity we have to give someone hope in God's miraculous working power. I have seen in my own life both of these circumstances when we were about to lose our house. In the beginning the giving of the people God sent into our lives increased our faith in an always hearing God. However, as the trial lingered we had a choice to make; to move forward or to wait on another deliverance through man. I will say it is very easy to just hope for man to supply the continual need, but in doing so we will never experience the excitement of seeing God do great things through our lives.

I tell a story of an avid couponer with a heart for helping the local food banks. So much so that she heads to the store on the first day of the sale and clears the shelves of all the coupon deals she is able to find. She saves some for her family and then she loads up the rest and takes it down to the local food bank. Shortly thereafter, a mother of three small children who has a $20 budget to feed her family on this week has also taken her coupons to the store. You see she has been able to take this blessing and stretch it to feed her family for yet another week. Sadly when she arrives she finds nothing left and in tears leaves the store and stops by the local food bank.

Often our good deed can create more need than good. It is so important to pray and ask God what you should give.

Determine for your life what you would comfortably like to live on. Through prayer, then decide where and how to distribute the surplus God gives you. In doing this you will be able to enjoy the blessings of wealth in your life and be giving out of your blessings to provide for the encouragement of God's people. This will in turn cause them to see an all powerful, hearing, answering, and delivering God who desires them to also search out their gifts for success.

Think about this—if we choose to give grudgingly, how much will God give us OR if we choose to over give how much will God give us? Either one can cost the success of someone else.

Giving prayerfully with a heart of love is a key to success and one that should be taught to our children. When we teach our children to give thankfully we will be teaching them to live thankfully.

Love Abundantly

Give Prayerfully

Receive Richly

CHAPTER 7

Marketing Your Gift

Marketing your product or service is crucial to the success of your business. Unless people know about your product or service it will most likely never achieve the power it has to change your life.

In this chapter I want to look at several tools you can use to create popularity and creditability for your product or service. Before we do this though, let's see if God's Word tells us anything about marketing. Is marketing a man-made tool or did marketing originate with God. What does the term "marketing" actually refer to?

Marketing is the commercial processes involved in promoting, selling and distributing something.

We look in John 1 to find the story of John the Baptist. God sent John the Baptist to "prepare the way for what was to come (Jesus) by telling of what He would do for man. We might say John was Jesus' marketer.

"There came a man sent by God, whose name was John, This man was to witness and testify of the Light, that all men might believe in it through him."
John 1:6-7

The message Bible says, "to show everyone where to look and who to believe in." The mission of John was make the people ready to receive Jesus. Marketing is telling people what is coming, where to find it and how it will benefit their lives. So you see God does believe in marketing.

In preparation as a marketer, John followed a radical lifestyle making sure he lived above reproach by abstaining from many of the world's ways and committing himself to study and work. There are many ways in which we can market our product or service, but all should be done in an honest way that does not bring reproach. Our marketing should consist of an honest evaluation of what we have and what it will do for those who choose to buy it.

Let's take a look at some of the popular ways to market a product or service that have proven their successfulness:

Test Marketing-This is one of the easiest ways to develop a demand for your product. Test marketing is simply creating an excitement about your product by giving it to friends, family members, coworkers etc.. to use and determine it's benefits. People who try your product or use your service can evaluate how it has helped them and make you aware of any thing that might help improve it's ability to meet their needs more efficiently. Test Marketing is offered free to individuals in exchange for testimonials about your product or service. Always get permission from the person to use their written testimonial concerning your product or service. Be sure they are okay with you using it in print, internet, and all other marketing aspects. One way to introduce your product or service might be to do a product unveiling. Prepare an event (you can post it on eventbrite for free) and do a Powerpoint presentation highlighting your product or service. Eventbrite is a free resource to help you advertise your event.

Another good area to test market to is well-known people who might have an interest in your product or service. Let's say for instance you have written a book and want the review of this well-known person. Send them a copy and ask them if they would please review it and again get permission to use their testimonial in public marketing.

Blogging and Mircroblogging-A blog is a great way to get the word out about your product. A blog is simply a shared on-line journal where people post about their personal experience, product, service and /or hobbies. People can leave comments to the post you make regarding your product or service. Most blogs will allow you to review and accept the comment before it posts online. Some web builders are set up with blog capability within their programs. However, some popular blogs are Word Press and Blogger. Another popular blog is Twitter. Twitter is what we call a mircoblogoger. Basically this means the posts are limited to a maximum word limit of 140 characters or less, whereas others will usually allow as many characters as you wish. Blogging allows the community to talk about what you've got. The more positive posts you have on your blog the more visibility your product or service will have.

Social Networks-These will include Facebook, Linkedin and MySpace as some of the most popular. Facebook will be a great way to get your friends on board with spreading your product as they connect with others. Linkedin is a tool for the business professional. Set up a Linkedin account with indepth information about your experience as well as testimonials from those who have worked with you for creditability. Linkedin is basically your portfolio to other business professionals. MySpace is similar to Facebook in the aspect you can connect with friends who will also connect with friends and grow your outreach. Both Facebook and MySpace are invaluable to get people sharing about what you do. For example if you have a flooring business and you just put in a floor for a client—connect with them on Facebook and ask them to make a post. They might say something like, "Wow, I love my new flooring. It is so easy to take care of. John Doe's Flooring sure got it done quickly." You would be surprised at the how quickly positive feedback spreads to potential clients.

Article Distribution-Another good way to spread the word about what you do is to write a story about it and send it to magazines with similar interest as a story submission. I have found that magazines are always looking for people who want to submit information. This helps them grow their readers and helps you promote your product. One online site you can check out for promoting your product is Squidoo. It is a free site for creating single webpages on your recommendations, product, or services.

Video Marketing-This is one area you definitely don't want to leave out. YouTube is a great source for getting your product attention. There are many who offer their services as videographers who can put together a timely, professional video of your product or service. Most can add graphics, music, editing, name and website inclusion as well. One to check out for all your video needs is Classamedia.com. Try and include live testimonials of those who have tried and love your product or services. These do not have to be live interviews, but this does help if at all possible. Videographers can create videos to meet your specific needs. Many well-known people have been discovered on Youtube as a result of posting videos of their talent.

Press Releases-A press release is simply a statement prepared for distribution to the news media announcing something claimed as having news value with the intent of gaining media coverage. Press Releases give you a professional creditability to your business. One press release site that is free is PRLOG.com. The site will give you details on writing a press release and you will be able to view other press releases as well.

Attend Vendor Fairs or Expos-A great exposure can be reached through setting up at these events as a vendor. Most will have a fee for the booth rental. Typically fairs fall on a Friday or Saturday and most will be at least an all day event. The amount of traffic these draw is usually phenomenal. Most are trade specific. For instance, if you are gun salesman you would want to attend a Gun Expo as a vendor. Search online to see where these shows are located. Preparation for your booth should have 3 important ingredients. Your booth should be informative, innovative, and independent. Informative refers to having brochures, business cards, flyers, and if possible a handout on something of interest around your trade. For example, if guns is your trade, a handout on gun safety might be a good way to get something in the hands of the attendees. Be sure to include your business name, website and contact information on all handouts. Innovation should give your interested attendees examples of how this product or service is like nothing they have seen before. Visual aids of before and after pictures or an illustrated aid might help with this.

Create a website-A website is crucial to all busineses today. Even if your service is not purchased online, a website gives a legitimacy of your business. A website should be eye catching, but not overwhelming. Search the internet for web designers if you need help in this area. Web designers can help you get a domain name for your website and will take care of hosting the website online.

Media Coverage-News media are always looking for fresh stories. If you have something that is helping others that would make for a great story contact them and see if they are interested. Let me give you an example. I present hundreds of motivational coupon presentations a year. What I teach helps people save money and efficiently manage their households. I contacted the local news letting them know what I do and this step turned into a series of features on the local news. One thing I always say is this, "Questioning is power." If you don't ask you won't know.

Radio Coverage-Talk radio shows are a great way to tell people what you do and how it can change their life for the better. An important thing to know about many radio stations is many are required to do public service announcements (PSA's). If you have something that would fall in line with a service to the community, you might want to see what their guidelines are on this. Contact them to see if they do PSA's and if so send them one and follow up a few days later with the program director. Make your announcement standout, for instance, "Would you like to learn to save hundred's of dollars off your grocery bill?" Even those who don't do PSA's are often a good avenue to try because they are generally looking for fresh ideas to entice their listeners.

Sponsorship– A sponsor is generally someone who supports what you do through some means of finances. They will often sponsor you in exchange for access to your clients. Let me explain. For instance, if you have a product or service they think will be a niche market, they may offer to do giveaway drawings to entice your market. In exchange for these giveaways they will generally collect a list of email names from the drawing slips to further promote their business. Most will also pay you a set amount for the opportunity to partner with you in this form of advertising. Keep in mind you will only want to work with those companies you believe in and those that are willing to benefit your business as well. Your customers are your first concern and you want to be sure that when your sponsor contacts them they will leave a positive impact on your customer.

Product Submission-Once you have developed your business it is important to grow your business through other business resources. Because you are a fairly new business it will take time for your product or service to gain recognition. It is quite helpful to submit your product or service through an already established business for the purpose of notability. For instance, you have a new book. Try taking your book to local book stores, video stores, etc.. to see if they would be interested in taking these on a trial run. You might start out asking them to put five in their store and giving them the option to pay you when they sell. I did this with my very first book. I took it to a local Christian book store and they agreed to try it out. I gave them a contract between them and myself stating the number of books given, date and signatures of both parties. Every two weeks they sent me a check for the books sold and I supplied them with more. You will also benefit from contacting larger online businesses. Now let me mention here some large businesses require financial statements of the business for a specified time period. If you are just getting going this will not be an avenue you can usually jump right into. However, many larger businesses will buy your product, especially if it is in line with something else they carry. Before submitting your product you will need to create a professional portfolio of it. There are several things that would be beneficial to include in your portfolio of your item.

Product Portfolio:

Cover Letter of Submission— on business letterhead announce your product, what it will do for customers, what it will do for their business, contact information.

Business card—should include your website, phone, address, slogan, logo.

Brochure—3 part brochure telling details of your product. There are many online templates you can use to create a professional looking brochure. Be sure to print these out on gloss paper for a rich appearance.

Wholesale Pricing Sheet—should include the price per piece for the retailer, the suggested retail price (personally, I would specify this to be priced no lower than the suggested price you give), payment options (ex. Net 30 days, due on receipt, etc…)

Copy of Your Product (if possible)—this will give the potential retailer a good idea of what to expect.

Some helpful websites for business basics are:

www.sba.gov—This is the site for the U.S. small business administration. Here you can get information about business licenses and permits.

www.uspto.gov—This website will help you with trademarks and patents.

www.isbn.org—Here you will be able to purchase an ISBN number for your book. This is a number that will identify the book as a unique title and allow for more opportunities in marketing to businesses, book sellers, wholesalers and distributors.

Finally, the most important thing about marketing is stepping out and trying even if you are not familiar with these types of marketing procedures. Many times we learn and improve as we. Have you ever noticed how books will sometimes say "revised version?" This is because they have often been upgraded to include more information or made editorial changes. We all learn as we go, but until we move into action we can never see where we need to improve. Don't let fear stop progress and don't let lack of expertise hinder trying. I have been in business since 2001 and have made many mistakes along the way. I have found ways to improve things, to make them more successful, and have found certain things didn't work at all. You've got to remember God placed the gift and He plans to finish the good work He starts in you. Don't let your gift die from lack of trying.

"Being confident of this, that He who began a good work in you will carry it on to completion until the day of Christ Jesus."
Phil. 1:6

Notice, the work had to begin.

Use What You Have

Learn What You Don't

Try What You Haven't

Improve Where You Can

Continue The Work

CHAPTER 8

What is the Status Of Your Gift

Active, Dormant, Extinct

Are you still wondering if your gift is functioning in an active way to produce it's full potential. Maybe at times you feel your gift has lost it's hope of producing great things. You might even be wondering if your gift has become extinct throughout the years of searching and hoping.

In this chapter you are going to learn about the stages our gifts can fall into and what factors play a part in the position of these gifts. First of all, let me reiterate that you still possess a gift even if you are not currently using it.

In order to better understand the stages of the gift we will apply an illustrated comparison of these gifts to the stages of a volcano.

A volcano typically has three stages in which it can exist: Active, Dormant, and Extinct. Now, let me say the volcano itself is still an actual structure, as is your gift regardless of the capacity it is functioning in. Let's take a look at the definition of each of the three stages the volcano can exist in:

Active: Volcanoes that erupt regularly, possessing an energy that can cause them to erupt at any time.

Dormant: Inactive, but capable of becoming active, sleeping, possessing unused power.

Extinct: Permanently inactive, having grown cold.

Here are some interesting facts about the three categories of volcanoes:

> 1500 are active [1]
> 50-60 actively erupt yearly[1]
> 9 are dormant[3]
> 5,000 are extinct[2]

Notice that most are either active or extinct. Very few are actually classified as dormant. Once a volcano becomes inactive it rarely becomes active again, thus causing it to become extinct. This is where many people today are with their gifts. They have the ability to use them possessing power but are sleeping. So many people today do not realize the ability they have to erupt into success. They have simply fallen asleep from weariness in trying to stir their gift up. This is a dangerous position to be in because it often leads to extinction.

Notice the 5000 that are extinct. Many people will fall in this category. This does not mean their gift doesn't exist, but rather it is permanently inactive, they have not used their gift in so long that it has become cold. These are the people who have completely lost hope in activating their gift for success. The discouragement of life's challenges have damaged their desire to once again stir this gift up. Think about the many lives this person might have touched including their own if they had not grown cold. There is truly nothing sadder than someone who has settled for a life of poverty due to unused gifts. Notice those that are active are 1500, how-

[1])http://www.ucl.ac.uk/EarthSci/people/sammonds/Descriptions_files/Volcanic%20eruptions.pdf
[2])http://wiki.answers.com/Q/How_many_extinct_volcanoes_in_the_world
[3])http://wiki.answers.com/Q/How_many_volcanoes_are_dormant_in_the_world

ever, only 50 –60 will erupt yearly. What can we see from this? They all possess the energy, however, only 50-60 will use it to actually erupt. What a small percentage we see of those who will actually use the energy they possess to surface an explosion of life changing flow. I want to be in this percentage, how about you? Do you desire to use your energy in conjunction with your gift to change the direction of your life?

What ingredients are seen in all of these types of volcanoes that make them equal as far as ability:

In an active volcano:

The place where everything gets started is below the surface in the magma chamber. We could refer to this as the place where God has placed our gift. Our gift resides within the very core of us. He has positioned a gift hot and ready for use. The gift is waiting for us to stir it up and create enough energy to spring it into action. When the plates below the earth's surface are stretched it can cause the magma to travel through the pipe toward the vent. This is very similar to what happens in our life. Many times it is not until we are stretched do we actually look for ways to bring our gift to the surface. We get tired of where we are and look for ways to produce change. This is when God stretches us to look for ways to change our lives. We start by making a heart decision to believe in the gift. Once the magma is pressurized it begins to rise up the pipe and out the vent where it expels from the crater. (The vent is where our heart meets our mind and convinces us it's time for action.) Finally the crater expels the hot lava, ash, and other material that changes the vicinity of things around it. (Here we bring to action the ideas, designs, products, services, etc... to change the circumstances sur-rounding our life.)

In an extinct volcano:

Something interesting to note, is as long as the plate remains in contact with the magma source the volcano will remain active. However, when the plate moves away from this hotspot the magma source is cut off and becomes extinct. God is our magma (gift) source and when we move away from Him, it disables our ability to bring forth an explosion of our gift for success. Our gift can only surface as long as we are in contact with the magma source (God). When we grow cold we lose our ability to succeed. At this point the volcano is only a shell of what used to be or could have been. A volcano might also be-come extinct when an eruption is so violent that the whole structure is blown away. This can often be a reference to someone who jumped out in excite-ment with their gift and didn't realize the time it would take to grow it and became discouraged. Im-patience then gave way to defeat. This is a very common occurrence. Remember the large number of extinct volcanoes. This is also where many people are at.

In a dormant volcano:

Some volcanoes become dormant due to the Earth's

plates constantly shifting above the hotspot. As the plates continue shifting above the hotspot the volcano becomes shut off from the magma chamber below. The volcano cannot erupt once this happens and becomes dormant. The magma looks for another place to erupt forming a new volcano. This can relate to a shifting Christian, one who is constantly moving away from God. This person is not satisfied and steadfast for very long. Once their gift surfaces they are active for a time, but return to the sleeping state. They move from one thing to another never fully developing into one successful being. They continually go a new direction when they hit a conflict. The dormant gift could also be one that is a hobby that never develops into a successful business. It is surfaced only in free time for enjoyment, but never reaching it's full potential.

Many people fall in this category. They know what their gift is, they even do it frequently, but they never use it to make life changes.

The important thing to remember about a gift that is active and erupting is this—it has the power to immediately affect everything and everyone in it's vicinity. As a matter of fact a powerful erupting volcano can affect aircrafts many miles away. Large eruptions can also affect the temperature of the air. Just think of the power your gift has when you use it. It can virtually change the course of your life and the lives of others.

Notice one other ingredient in every volcano, the cone. The cone is a layering of lava and ash built up from past eruptions. This is what defines the way a volcano appears. What can you see from your past eruptions of using your gift? How is your appearance? Have past experiences with using your gift brought positive change to your life and those around you? It is important that we reflect on what God has done in our past to encourage our trust in Him for our future. You see, building the cone is not an overnight task and neither is building our success. We will rise as we continually allow our gift to surface and erupt into great things by the energy God puts in us and the opportunities He allows to come our way.

So I ask you: What is the status of your gift? Is your gift Active (currently changing your life and the lives of others)? Is your gift Dormant (sleeping with a storage of unused power)? Is your gift Extinct (having grown cold and doubtful of resurfacing?

My hope is that you will reach deep inside and draw your strength from God to stir up the gift once again and allow God to do mighty things through your life and the lives of others. It's never too late to unleash the entrepreneur inside you. The only way to fail is to never try again.

"That is why I remind you to STIR UP the gift of God that is in you…"
2 Timothy 1:6

Stir up means to bring into action or existence. Action refers to the operating part that transmits power to a mechanism. In other words God is telling us to summon our gifts forth so they can transmit power to change our lives. Our gifts are sure to bring about success. How do I know this? Proverbs 18:16 says,

"A man's gift makes room for him and brings him before great men."

Look with me at the life of Abigail in 1 Samuel 25. Here her selfish husband refuses to give to David and his men. Abigail realizing that her wicked husband had brought about evil upon her household gathers a gift and takes it to David asking that he disregard Nabal's foolishness. Abigail states,

"And now this gift, which your handmaid has brought my lord, let it be given to the young men who follow my lord."
1 Samuel 25:27

You see Abigail understood that a gift possessed was to be given in love to the benefit of others and the security of one's self. If this gift had remained in the hands of Nabal, destruction would have come to their household. Instead, the gift used brought success.

Every gift from God in a person's life has a purpose to fulfill great things for God. When used God brings blessing to His people. When left unused we may never know what would have been.

Don't be left wondering. Activate your gift and experience an overflow of success in your life.

CHAPTER 9

Staying In Business
And Finishing Well

Financial success with happiness is rooted in three important keys: Starting well, staying well, and finishing well. Have you ever wondered why some Christian businesses get off to a great start, but end up closing their doors after a few short years? Maybe you've wondered why other people are successful in business when they don't honor God? Let me explain something very important. Financial success and material wealth in itself will never satisfy man. Man was meant to honor God and without honor the appearance of their lifestyle may seem enjoyable, however I can assure you their wealth is not sufficient to make them happy. This is why we see so many who end up on drugs, alcohol, and in promiscuous lifestyles looking for something they do not have. It is sad to say that these could be successful lives are often brought into turmoil and unhappiness. Solomon's life is a perfect example of this. He was a man who had it all—the favor of God, wisdom, riches, yet He grew cold towards God in his pursuits for fleshly desires. His wealth was never able to satisfy him. He concludes that man's efforts must be God-focused not self-focused if joy is to be found.

But, what about those who honor God yet fail in business? Understand this, God desires that we enjoy the fruit of our labors and achieve financial success. It is quite sad to see those who claim personal happiness without financial success is enough. Let me ask you a question; do you want only half of what God wants you to have? God desires to give you success in all areas of your life not just part of it.

Financial success is a God-given principle not a man-made plan. Unfortunately, most people will fall into one of two categories: those who achieve financial success but lack personal happiness or those who have personal happiness but lack financial success.

I am sure you are reading this book because you want everything God has for you, which is both. It is my hope that by the time you reach the end of this chapter you will have discovered how to experience abundance in both of these areas.

Once we discover our gift and begin to use it we will notice the gift is beneficial to not only ourselves, but those around us. This is the first purpose of your gift—giving it to God for His use. Starting well means letting God have complete control of the gift He gives you. This means putting Him and His wishes above your own in every area especially with your gifts. Only a gift sacrificed will be a successful and fulfilling gift. Think about Abraham for a moment, he after 25 years received the fulfillment of the gift God had promised Him (Isaac, his son.) Later sometime when Isaac was thought to be about 25 years old Abraham was asked to sacrifice him to God, which he began to follow out. God intervened and stated,

"...because you have gone through with this and have not refused to give me your son, your dear, dear son, I'll bless you—oh, how I'll bless you! And I'll make sure that your children flourish—like stars in the sky, like sand on the beaches! And your

descendants will defeat their enemies. All nations
on Earth will find themselves blessed through your
descendants because you obeyed me."
Genesis 22:16-18

Note that Abraham's obedience to God regarding his gift carried abundant blessing with it. When Abraham gave his gift to God, God gave it back to him with greater blessing. God will always ask us to sacrifice what He gives us to determine our commitment to Him and His purpose for our gift.

I have experienced this several times in my life. After we lost our home God asked us to make a move in our life in order to see His purpose fulfilled. This meant we were to leave Illinois and move to Tennessee. I struggled greatly with this because my family was from Illinois, my children were born there and I knew leaving would mean starting over. I especially struggled with the fact that my children's lives would not be what I thought was best, stability and family roots. God began to deal with me on this. I often compare myself to Jacob wrestling with God all night long. I gave God every reason this was not a good idea, however my efforts to convince Him were of no avail. I'll never forget what I heard in my spirit, "Do you not know I love your children more than you do and would never do anything that would destroy their future?" This was the winning question. Obedience was the only answer.

"Jesus said, Truly I tell you, there is no one who has
given up and left house or brothers and sisters and
mothers and children and lands, for my sake and

the Gospels who will not receive a hundred times as much now in this time—houses and brothers and sisters and mothers and children and lands, with persecutions-and in the age to come, eternal life."
Mark 10:29-30 [AMP]

I started the book with this scripture, but it's worth repeating. God will ask us to surrender those things He has given us in order to give them back to us in greater capacity. After moving to Tennessee the opportunities and success of my children have been evident. Two of my sons own businesses (at the age of 18 and 24) and my other children are receiving opportunities only God could have known were waiting for them. Notice it tells us God gives us a hundred times as much now in this time (in Luke 18:30 it says "in this world.") Also, notice because of Abrahams obedience God gave even more blessing through his gift (Isaac). I cannot express to you how important it is to trust God with what He gives you from the littlest to the most important thing in your life. You will always find, especially in finances God will require a sacrifice from you. He desires to see what is more important to you. We cannot serve God and money (Matthew 6:24) If you desire to get your business started well, let God be in control of the finances. When you give them to Him without reserve He gives them back to you in abundance.

Notice in Mark 10:30 it says "with persecution." This is not the most pleasant part of the blessing. Abraham was persecuted of spirit when he was asked to sacrifice Isaac. Can you imagine the questioning, suffering and even fear he probably experienced? You will face a persecution of your mind through questioning and fear and a persecution of your flesh of self-desire. I will be honest with you in telling you that the giving of your dreams and gifts will be the hardest part to starting well in business. Only a sacrificed dream can become a resurrected reality. I assure you through much tears I have come to understand that God does know best and has my best interest in mind. Too doubt this will delay the birth of your gift and your dream for financial freedom.

Many circumstances will arise to challenge your successfulness. But how you handle the challenge will determine the outcome.

*"..not that I was in personal want, for I have learned how to be content (satisfied to the point where I am not disturbed or disquieted) in whatever state I am. I know how to be abased and live humbly in straitened circumstances and I know also how to enjoy plenty and live in abundance. I have learned in any and all circumstances the secret of facing every situation, whether well-fed or going hungry, having a sufficiency and enough to spare or going without and being in want. I HAVE STRENGTH FOR ALL THINGS IN CHRIST WHO EMPOWERS ME (I AM READY FOR ANYTHING AND EQUAL TO ANYTHING THROUGH HIM WHO INFUSES INNER STRENGTH INTO ME. I AM SELF-SUFFICIENT IN CHRIST'S SUFFICIENCY."
Phil. 4:11-13*

We must learn the secret to facing our challenges in life whether in business, family, or any aspect of life is to be content drawing our strength from Christ. Does this mean we are to be satisfied with the challenges and not proactive in looking for solutions? Absolutely not! What it does mean is that our circumstances should not change our belief and confidence that God will deliver us into a victory. Many people will quit when the challenges arrive and miss out on the victory. To encounter the victory we must remain in the fight and look for the answers of opportunity God gives us to change our situation and improve our circumstances.

Don't go back to bondage! In 1 Samuel 8 the Israelites did not like the way things were going and demanded a king to rule over them. Samuel told them of the bondage and all a king would require of them including much of their belongings, however, they insisted saying we want someone to fight our battles and we want to be like the other nations. If you spend too much time trying to avoid fighting your own battles and being like everyone else you will never fulfill the call God has placed on your life through your individual gift. God does not remove His call just because you have removed your desire to fulfill it. Your life will be the story of a success that could have been.

"For God's gifts and His call are irrevocable. [He never withdraws them once they are given and He does not change His mind about those to whom He gives His grace or to whom He sends His call."
Romans 11:29

In this one statement your success will be assured—Build your business on Christ allowing Him to be the CEO of your life. The CEO responsibilities are defined as —The highest ranking executive in a company whose main responsibilities include developing and implementing high-level strategies, making major corporate decisions, managing the overall operations and resources of a company, and acting as the main point of communication between the board of directors and the corporate operations. God has your business' best interest in mind and will communicate his direction to you for all business decisions. He must be the foundation to endure the trials that come with all businesses.

"These words I speak to you are not incidental additions to your life, homeowner improvements to your standard of living. They are foundational words, words to build a life on. If you work these words into your life, you are like a smart carpenter who built his house on solid rock. Rain poured down, the river flooded, a tornado hit—but nothing moved that house. It was fixed to the rock."

Matthew 7:24-25[AMP]

There are no shortcuts to building. A successful business will take time to construct, but it is worth the time to stay secure.

"Don't look for shortcuts to God. The market is flooded with surefire, easy-going formulas for a successful life that can be practiced in your spare time.

Don't fall for that stuff, even though crowds of people do. The way to life—to God!—is vigorous and requires total attention."
Matt. 7:13-14

Get rich quick schemes will lead to failure, but get God quick plans will lead to the formula for success you have been looking for.

Now we understand what it takes to start well in business and virtually any endeavor in life. We have seen that continued dependency on God when challenges hit will help us overcome, but what about when things are sailing along smoothly? Is there anything to be concerned about during these times? Unfortunately there is!

One of the most common failures in business occurs when people forget where they came from. Man has a tendency to depend on God to get financial prosperity going then forget Him once the increase is flowing. In 1 Samuel 12:8-11 Samuel reminds the people of their past patterns. He tells them God sent Moses and Aaron when they were afflicted by the Egyptians, once God brought them out they forgot Him. The people began to live life without concern for God, forgetting where He had brought them from. When this happens it will always lead back to bondage. Always remember why you are where you are once you establish business success and thank God for it continually. It might help to make the anniversary of your business a dedication to God once a year with a time of remembering and celebrating His success through you.

Look what happened to Saul when he worked in his own will and forgot the will of God in 1 Sam 15:17-19,

"When you were small in your own sight, were you not made the head of the tribes of Israel, and the Lord anointed you king over Israel? And the Lord sent you on a mission and said, Go...Why then did you not obey the voice of the Lord, but swooped down upon the plunder…."

It is generally those who have entered the comfort zone and the enjoyment of material wealth that will find it hardest to stay committed to God. Saul's decision to keep the plunder in this case cost him his throne. You see it is not God who has changed, but rather the heart of man that costs him his success. This is why the scripture tells us in Matthew 19:24,

"..it is easier for a camel to go through the eye of a needle than for a rich man to go into the kingdom of heaven."

This is why we often see Christian businesses fail. When money or the pleasures of money become more important than the call God has placed on our life we will lose our ability to succeed.

Finally, how can we be assured to finish well?

1. Don't despise the small beginnings.

"..you have been faithful and trustworthy over a

little; I will put in you in charge of much."
Matt. 25:21

2. Learn as much as you can

*"It takes wisdom to build a house, and understand-
ing to set it on a firm foundation; it takes knowledge to furnish its rooms with fine furniture and
beautiful draperies."*
Prov. 24:3-4

3. Be hungry for the gift of God working in your life

*"Appetite is an incentive to work; hunger makes
you work all the harder."*
Prov 16:26

4. Stay busy

*"Who here qualifies for the job of overseeing the
kitchen? A person the Master can depend on to feed
the workers on time each day. Someone the Master
can drop in on unannounced and always find him
doing his job. A God-blessed man or woman I tell
you! It won't be long before the Master will put this
person in charge of the whole operation."*
Matt 24:45-47 [AMP]

5. Work Hard

*"Committed and persistent work pays off; get rich
quick schemes are rip-offs."*
Prov 28:20 [AMP]

6. Be God -minded not world-minded

"I'm not trying to get my way in the world's way. I'm trying to get Your way, Your Word's way."
Psalm 17:4 [AMP]

7. Give to God

"Bring all the tithes into the storehouse, that there may be food in My house, and prove Me now by it...see if I don't open the windows of heaven for you and pour out a blessing that there shall not be room enough to receive it."
Malachi 3:10

8. Be honest in your business

"God cares about honesty in the workplace; your business is his business."
Prov 16:11

9. Don't trust in riches

"The rich think their wealth protects them; they imagine themselves safe behind it. Pride first, then the crash, but humility is precursor to honor."
Prov. 18:11-12

10. Always remain humble

"Humility and fear of the Lord bring wealth, honor and life."
Prov. 22:4

11. Give to others

"The one who blesses others is abundantly blessed; those who help others are helped."
Prov 11:25

12. Pay your taxes

"Pay to Caesar the things that are Caesar's and to God the things that are God's."
Mark 12:17

These twelve tips are what I believe to be the most important things we can do to assure the success God wants us to have in the present and the future.

It is up to us as to whether or not we take God at His word. We must remember success was God's idea and we can't achieve it without Him. I remind myself daily of my need for total dependence on God for success in everything in my life, from my family to my ministry and business. I have not achieved because of what I can do, but rather because of what God has chosen to do through me. I know that God desires to do great things through your life as well and will if you trust Him to do the work. He desires to start and finish a success story in your life as well. What God has done for me He wants to do for you.

"..If you embrace the way God does things, there are wonderful payoffs, again without regard to where you are from or how you were brought up."
Romans 2:11 [AMP]

God never started a job He couldn't finish. God placed the gift in you and is ready to unleash it for success. Are you ready to give Him control of your life and your gift and lay aside your plan for His? I can assure you His plan will bring you more than you ever dreamed of!

"Who got things rolling here...Who recruited him for his job...Who did this? Who made it happen? Who always gets things started? I did. GOD! I'm the first on the scene. I'm also the last to leave."
Isaiah 41:2,3,4

About the Author

Ann Haney has been involved in motivational public speaking since 1999. She is a wife of 20+ years and home schooling mother of 6 children for 15+ years. She has been an entrepreneur since 2001. She is CEO of Aaron Publishing and founder of Ann Haney Ministries, author and publisher of 19 products including 5 year best seller "Homeschool Daily Planner for Curriculum." Ann has spoken in 7 different states on various topics.

She has been featured on Nashville Fox 17 news several times for her money saving techniques. Also, Ann has been on 760 AM The Gospel with Renee Bobb Empowerment for Women talk radio and WLAC in Nashville with Devon O'Day & Kim McLean Plain Jane Wisdom talk radio. Ann's newspaper coverage includes: The Tennessean, Leaf Chronicle, DNJ, Shelbyville Times Gazette (where she was a weekly columnist in 2011), Illinois Alliant, Upside of Money "Faith & Finance", and The Nashville Examiner (where she is currently a weekly columnist) Her goal is helping people uncover their resources and team them up with their God-given potential to achieve success.

Ann has conducted hundreds of motivational presentations for women's conferences, businesses, churches, organizations, life enrichment teachings, lunch & learns, schools, wellness programs, Goodwill industries Career Centers Fort Campbell, VA Recovery, Nutrition Programs, Banks and more.

If you are interested in having Ann speak at an event contact her at ann@annhaney.com

You may view Ann's products and speaking availability on her website at annhaney.com

Ann Haney ministries is a 501 (c) (3) non-profit organization.

Note From The Author

My prayer for you is that God speaks His will into your life and shows you the gift He has given you personally. I pray blessing and prosperity upon your life as you use your gift. May you always be abundant in wisdom, direction and finances to bring glory to God and a witness to others of God's love for His people.

If you do not know my God I invite you to give your heart to Him. Say this prayer and start experiencing a new life.

"Lord, I know I have broken your laws and my sins have separated me from you. I am sorry and I want to turn away from my past sinful life. Please forgive me. I believe your son, Jesus Christ died for my sins, was resurrected from the dead, is alive, and hears my prayer. I ask you to become Lord of my life, to rule and reign in my heart. Please help me obey You, and do Your will for the rest of my life. In Jesus' name I pray, Amen."